Winning Cooperation from Your Child!

REVISED EDITION

DEVELOPMENTS IN CLINICAL PSYCHIATRY

A Series of Books Edited by
Anthony L. LaBruzza, M.D.

The books in this series address various facets of the role of psychiatry in the modern world.

Using DSM-IV: *A Clinician's Guide to Psychiatric Diagnosis*
Anthony L. LaBruzza and José M. Méndez-Villarrubia

Filicide: *The Murder, Humiliation, Mutilation, Denigration, and Abandonment of Children by Parents*
Arnaldo Rascovsky

Return from Madness: *Psychotherapy with People Taking the New Antipsychotic Medications and Emerging from Severe, Lifelong, and Disabling Schizophrenia*
Kathleen Degen and Ellen Nasper

The Chambers of Memory: *PTSD in the Life Stories of U. S. Vietnam Veterans*
H. William Chalsma

Winning Cooperation from Your Child!
Revised Edition: *A Comprehensive Method to Stop Defiant and Aggressive Behavior in Children*
Kenneth Wenning

Brainstorms: *Understanding and Treating the Emotional Storms of Attention Deficit Hyperactivity Disorder from Childhood through Adulthood*
H. Joseph Horacek

Twisted: *Inside the Mind of a Drug Addict*
Carl Adam Richmond

The Essential Internet:
A Guide for Psychotherapists and Other Mental Health Professionals
Anthony L. LaBruzza

Building a Neuropsychology Practice:
A Guide to Respecialization
Marvin H. Podd and Donald P. Seelig

Men Are from Earth, Women Are from Earth:
A Guide to Winning Cooperation from Your Spouse
Kenneth Wenning

Winning Cooperation from Your Child!

REVISED EDITION

A COMPREHENSIVE METHOD TO STOP DEFIANT AND AGGRESSIVE BEHAVIOR IN CHILDREN

Kenneth Wenning, Ph.D.

JASON ARONSON INC.
Northvale, New Jersey
London

This book is not intended to be a substitute for diagnosis, treatment, or professional care rendered by a qualified child mental health professional.

Production Editor: Elaine Lindenblatt

This book was set in 12 pt. Garamond Light by Alpha Graphics of Pittsfield, New Hampshire and printed and bound by Book-mart Press of North Bergen, New Jersey.

Library of Congress Cataloging-in-Publication Data

Wenning, Kenneth.
    Winnind cooperation from your child! / by Kenneth Wenning. — Rev.
ed.
      p. cm.
    Includes bibliographical references.
    ISBN 0-7657-0231-2
    1. Problem children—Behavior modification. 2. Oppositional
defiant disorder in children. 3. Child rearing. 4. Parent and
child. I. Title.
HQ773.W45 1999
649'.64—dc21   99-28197

Printed in the United States of America on acid-free paper. For information and catalog write to Jason Aronson Inc., 230 Livingston Street, Northvale, New Jersey 07647-1726, or visit our website: www.aronson.com

To my son
Daniel

Contents

Preface to the Revised Edition   ix

Preface to the First Edition   xi

1   Getting Ready for Change   1

2   Are Your Parenting Attitudes
    Helpful or Harmful?   31

3   Positive Reinforcement Techniques   45

4   Penalties for Noncompliance, Defiance,
    and Aggression   69

5   Self-Control Skills, Part I: Building
    Thinking Skills   97

6   Self-Control Skills, Part II: Building
    Verbalization Skills   111

7   Self-Control Skills, Part III: Building
    Impulse-Control, Problem-Solving,
    and Tease-Tolerance Skills   131

8 Monitoring Progress   145

      Appendix: Guidelines for Clinicians   163

      Suggested Reading   175

      References   179

      Index   183

Preface to the Revised Edition

It has now been three years since *Winning Cooperation from Your Child!* was first published. Many parents welcomed this book because it gave them crucial information about childhood defiance and aggression as well as concrete strategies that they could use to help their children become more cooperative and less aggressive. Since that time I have continued to learn newer and even more effective ways to help defiant children overcome their problems and experience the pleasures and benefits of cooperative life with others. This revised and expanded second edition contains much of what I have learned or developed in recent years as well as many refinements to material presented in the first edition. The book is now based on my nearly twenty years of experience with oppositional children and their families and on a wide range of published research by other investigators. Throughout each of its eight chapters I have synthesized this data in an effort to create an even more comprehensive and potent intervention for defiant children.

For help in the preparation of this revised edition I am grateful to a number of individuals. Many thanks go to Dr. Jason Aronson who first supported the idea to revise and update this book. I also thank Elaine Lindenblatt, Judith Tulli, Norma Pomerantz, and the entire staff at Jason Aronson Inc. Working collaboratively with this team of professionals is always a pleasure. I also want to express my appreciation, again, to my transcriptionist, Patricia Nann, for her assistance in preparing the manuscript. Finally I want to thank the many children and families I have encountered in my years of practice. I have indeed learned a great deal from them.

Preface to the First Edition

Does this sound familiar? Your child ignores your directions, talks back to you, picks on and hits his brother or sister, and has started to tell lies. When angered he slams doors, breaks or throws things, and won't take no for an answer. You have tried reasoning with him, yelling, threatening, spanking, and other punishments, and instead of doing better he is becoming even more difficult. You feel worn out from the daily battles with your child and have begun to think he is beyond your control.

Nothing seems to frustrate parents more than oppositional, defiant, and aggressive behavior in a child. Over the years many parents have been referred to me for consultation about such problems. Almost always, the most pressing question is, "What can we do to make our child behave?" This is a question to which I have given much thought. This book reflects my attempt to provide parents with an answer.

The child management method described in this book is designed to promote cooperative, nonaggressive behavior in children 2 to 11 years of age. The techniques described have been used with children diagnosed with Oppositional Defiant Disorder, Conduct Disorder, and Attention Deficit Hyperactivity Disorder. The techniques also work well with children who do not carry a formal diagnosis but who are nonetheless difficult and uncooperative.

Throughout each chapter I have integrated my ideas with what I regard as some of the best child management techniques and psychological strategies developed by a number of mental health professionals. Most notably, I am indebted to Joseph Strayhorn, M.D., Michael Bernard, Ph.D., Marie Joyce, Ph.D., Russell Barkley, Ph.D., Albert Ellis, Ph.D., Phillip Kendall, Ph.D., Lauren Braswell, Ph.D., Alan Kazdin, Ph.D., Michael Breen, Ph.D., Thomas Altepeter, Ph.D., Rex Forehand, Ph.D., Robert McMahon, Ph.D., Charles Huber, Ph.D., and Leroy Baruth, Ed.D. Their writings have significantly increased my ability to help defiant children and their parents.

A number of colleagues have reviewed portions of this book and provided me with feedback. For their help and encouragement I want to thank Leslie Pollack Wenning, MSW, Frank Ninivaggi, M.D., Jeff Summerville, MSW, Robert Koenig, Ph.D., Suzanne King, MSW, Morris Wessel, M.D., Alan Kazdin, Ph.D., and Pramila Nathan, M.D. I also thank Toni Nixon and Anne Bauerdorf for their encouragement and Patricia Nann for her skill in preparing the manuscript. Finally I want to thank Chet Brodnicki, MSW, and the rest of the staff at the Clifford W. Beers Guidance Clinic in New Haven, CT. Our years of collaboration on behalf of children and families have helped me to develop many of the ideas discussed in this book.

1

Getting Ready
for Change

This book is designed to give you accurate information about oppositional and defiant behavior in children and concrete strategies you can use to encourage your child to display greater self-control and more cooperative and flexible behavior. Although you may be in a hurry to get to the chapters that discuss ways to deal with your child's disobedience, I urge you to proceed slowly and to carefully read and contemplate the material in this and all subsequent chapters. The process of helping an oppositional child recover from months or years of disobedient behavior is just that—a process. By giving yourself time to understand, digest, and gradually implement the information and child management techniques in this book, you will be more likely to help your child grow and change in a more positive direction.

Two types of change need to occur for your child to give up his defiant and aggressive behavior. The first type of change is environmental change. Your attitudes, behaviors, rules, methods of discipline, and lifestyle constitute the environment in which your child lives. The material in this chapter and in Chapters 2 through 4 is designed to help you make whatever changes are necessary to create a recovery-oriented home environment for your defiant child. The second type of change that needs to occur involves altering the way your child solves problems and expresses thoughts and feelings so that he or she can begin to develop solid inner self-control skills. The final chapters of this book offer a variety of strategies you can use to help your child develop greater self-control and flexibility when confronted with day-to-day problems of living or difficult situations. The combination of home-based environmental change created by you, and inner change in your child created by you and your child working together as a team, often produces a more cooperative son or daughter.

The goal of this chapter and of Chapter 2 is to help you change your home into a recovery-oriented environment for your oppositional child. To prepare for this type of change you need to learn three facts about oppositional, defiant, and aggressive behavior in children; conduct a review of problems known to decrease the effectiveness of the behavior modification techniques discussed in Chapters 3 through 8; be aware of factors that sabotage or prevent change; know the causes of oppositional/defiant behavior; and learn four key social learning principles. This foundation of information is designed to be something like a "preflight" checklist for parents (see Table 1–1). If most of the following systems are "go," you will be well positioned to begin using the specific child management and skill building methods in this book. Let's get started.

TABLE 1-1. Parent "Preflight" Checklist

Review all of the topics on this page and note the ones you will need to start to improve upon before using the child management method in this book.

1. Commitment to child's need for help
2. Anger control
3. Role model
4. Personal problem
5. Optimism about child's future
6. Blaming others
7. Playfulness with child
8. Procrastination
9. Creating too many conflict points
10. Time for yourself
11. Understanding child's feelings
12. Hectic week problem
13. Fear of change
14. Not following a plan long enough
15. Causes of oppositional behavior
16. Nagging, threatening, screaming syndrome

Once you have started to make some headway in the areas you have identified, you are ready to move on. Also, be sure to review the four social learning principles discussed at the end of this chapter.

OPPOSITIONAL, DEFIANT, AND AGGRESSIVE BEHAVIOR IN CHILDREN

Fact #1—You can eliminate and reverse some of the possible causes of oppositional, defiant, and aggressive behavior in your child. Numerous factors contribute to the development of these behaviors. Inconsistent discipline, severe parental conflict, excessive punishment of the child, lack of parental supervision, inappropriate peer influence, angry adult role models, television violence, and difficult temperament in the child are just some of the suspected culprits. The good news, however, is that some of the factors that contribute to the development of oppositionality, defiance, and aggression in children are under parental control and can therefore be eliminated by parents if parents *choose* to do so.

Fact #2—The symptoms of oppositionality, aggression, and defiant attitude are very durable over time. In other words, oppositional, defiant, and aggressive behavior in children generally does not go away on its own. Without parental—and in many cases professional—intervention, oppositional, defiant, and aggressive children are at risk for much more serious future adjustment problems. Reports of outcome studies show that many chronically oppositional children later become involved in drug and alcohol abuse, sexual promiscuity, stealing, fighting, truancy, dropping out of school, and poor work and marital adjustment (Breen and Altepeter 1990).

Fact #3—Even with treatment and/or a home-based behavioral recovery program, some oppositional children remain oppositional, defiant, and aggressive. If your child does not respond to the methods in this book, consult a child mental health professional to discuss the possibility of a more intensive intervention for your child.

You are reading this book because you are obviously concerned about your child and his future. As you read the following pages, keep two facts in mind. Without some type of intervention, your child's behavior problems may well become worse. And because you are in control of some of the factors that may contribute to oppositional, defiant, and aggressive behavior in your child, you are in a *powerful* position to help him or her develop better behavioral, social, and attitudinal skills. But you may have to make some changes first.

PARENTS HAVE TO CHANGE FIRST

After years of working with children and families, I have learned that certain types of parental problems seriously interfere with efforts to help oppositional children function better. For this reason I want you to review the following nine questions. If you think any of the issues discussed below is a problem for you, do whatever you can to start to eliminate the problem or problems *before* using the techniques in this book. If you are doing well in the following areas, you are ready to move on to Chapter 2.

1. *Is your child's need for help your highest priority?* You may feel insulted that I have asked you to consider how your child's need for help compares to other

responsibilities. To be honest, I would rather risk your indignation than not ask the question. Take some time to review all of your current responsibilities and activities and, if necessary, reduce your commitments so that you have time each day to work with your child toward *real* behavioral improvement. If you haven't done so already, I recommend that you define your child's need for behavioral recovery as your highest priority and then act accordingly. Your child will not get better without a substantial investment of time and energy on your part.

2. *Is your anger under control?* If you are an overly angry parent you will create four major problems for yourself. First, your child will resent you and will find ways of fighting back with passive-aggressive behavior or active rebellion and defiance. Second, you will feel guilty about the harsh way you are treating your child. Third, you will be acting like the worst boss you have ever had—the one who was irritable, abrupt, demanding, and angry! Thus your child's motivation or desire to do a good job for you will be extremely low. Finally, your child will likely feel both scared and very powerful, because some children view parental anger as entertainment even though it also frightens them. If you need help managing your anger, read one of the anger-reducing self-help books listed at the end of this book or consult a therapist. The techniques you will learn in later chapters will not work if you use them in anger.

3. *Are you a role model for your child?* Perhaps you already know that all of your behavior and your attitudes constitute the first and most impressive "road map" for living that your child will use to navigate through life. For this reason it is critically important that you model the behaviors and attitudes that you want your child to display. Thus, if you want your child to be more cooperative, tolerant, honest, patient, gentle, and respectful, it is necessary for you to frequently display these behaviors and attitudes around your child. If your behavior does not match your stated expectations and rules, you will be sending mixed messages to your child. Children generally pay more attention to parental behavior than parental words. For example, I once counseled a parent who demanded that her son stop swearing even though she (the mother) liberally used obscene language at home and believed that this was permissible for adults. In this case the boy identified with his mother's behavior rather than his mother's stated rule about swearing. Other examples of parents sending mixed messages include spanking children to stop them from hitting; screaming at children to stop them from yelling defiantly at others; and displaying dishonest ideas, behaviors, and attitudes and expecting children to be honest.

4. *Do you have a problem that needs treatment?* This is a sensitive but necessary question. Certain types of psychiatric problems are known to interfere with parental efforts to help children improve their behavior. Spe-

cifically, serious depression or anxiety, personality problems, attention deficit/hyperactivity disorder, temper
problems, and/or drug and alcohol abuse are all likely
to interfere with your ability to consistently use the techniques in this book. Intense conflict with your spouse or
partner regarding child management strategies will also
make the use of my approach less effective. If you think
you may have a problem in one of these areas, seek a
comprehensive evaluation from a qualified mental health
professional. Getting yourself help may be the best gift
you could give yourself and your child.

5. *Are you optimistic about your child's future?* Hope-
fulness and optimism regarding your child's ability to
show behavioral improvement are critical. An optimistic
attitude tells your child that you know he or she has the
potential to do better and that you expect improvement
to occur at some point. By harnessing the power of positive thinking, you may be able to influence your child to
live up to your positive vision of his future. Thus, under
all circumstances, tell yourself that your child will be able
to do better with your continued support, encouragement,
and teaching.

6. *Do you create too many conflict points with your
child?* Parents who repeatedly say "No, don't do that" often
create unnecessary conflict points with their children. Try
to develop increased tolerance for some of your child's

minor behavioral troubles and/or his natural tendency to get into things. Carefully pick and choose your battles with your child. The simple technique of reducing the number of times that you say no during the day reduces the number of conflict points you and your child will experience. This often leads to the feeling that things are improving already.

7. *Are you playful with your child?* Playfulness and humor are very important to the mental health needs of parents and children and to the overall quality of the parent–child relationship. The more playful you can be with your child, the more likely it is that your child will want to cooperate with your rules and expectations. Good-natured humor, moderate doses of silliness, and a few belly laughs each day go a long way toward helping parents and children cope with those aspects of life that are really difficult.

8. *Do you have time for yourself?* Periodically you need to forget about children, bills, work, and all of life's hassles to refresh yourself. You will be less effective in managing your child if you are chronically worn out and irritable and do nothing but spend time in the trenches with children. Find a way to have some adult leisure time for yourself each day and each week. A stress-reduction plan for parents is an important aspect of my approach to helping oppositional children behave better.

9. *Do you know what your child is thinking and feeling right now?* Beneath that angry defiant attitude many oppositional children often have strong feelings of sadness and worry. My own research on a group of oppositional/defiant children revealed that close to 50 percent of the children I studied were also depressed or had features of depression (Wenning et al. 1993). Read the following letter I have written for parents on behalf of some of the oppositional children I have known.

Dear Mom and Dad:

I am very sad and mixed up right now. There is too much conflict and anger in our home. I wish that each of you could find a way to be less angry and upset. I also wish that you could be nicer to each other. I know that I give you a hard time and I wish I could stop, but often it's easier to stir up trouble than to think about how sad and worried I am about what is going on in our family. I don't think I can change until I see that you have changed and until it feels safe to change. All the anger makes it hard for me to talk about my behavior and my feelings. Please show me with your words and your actions how to constructively solve our problems and how to make our home a less angry place. If you can show me the way, I'll try real hard to improve my behavior and my attitude.

Love,
Your Child

FACTORS THAT WORK AGAINST CHANGE

Change is not easy even under the best of circumstances. Below are five major factors that commonly sabotage parental efforts to implement an effective child management plan. If any of the following obstacles to change is potentially a problem for you, actively develop a plan to overcome it. Remember, your child's future is at stake!

1. *Procrastination*—Procrastination is the tendency to delay repeatedly or to continuously put off doing something until some future date—which never arrives! Procrastination is often based on the unhelpful idea that a task is simply too hard to start or to complete. When you say that something is too hard, you are really saying "impossibly hard," as if someone had just asked you to move Mount Rushmore from South Dakota to Texas. Rather than say it is too hard to start and maintain a new child management play today, say: "It will be very hard for me to start today but *not too hard.*" If you can change your thinking in this way, you will be better able to fight procrastination. For further help in this area read one of the self-help books on procrastination that I have listed at the end of this book.

2. *The "hectic week" problem*—This is mainly a form of procrastination but it comes up so often in my practice that I want to discuss the issue separately. Many times

after I start to train parents in how to use the techniques in this book, they fail to begin using them at home or start to use them but stop because "it's been such a hectic week." If you find yourself letting your child management plan slide because you had a busy week, ask yourself, "Is my child's recovery my main priority?" and "How will my child's behavior improve if I am not actively working with him each day toward that goal?" By excusing your failure to start and maintain the use of the techniques in this book on the basis of things being "hectic," you are procrastinating and/or have not made a decision to make your oppositional child's need for help your highest priority.

3. *Blaming your child or your child's other parent—* Blaming your oppositional child or your child's other parent will get you nowhere fast in your search for solutions to your child's behavioral and attitudinal difficulties. Blaming others and demanding that they act differently really reflects your godlike attempt to change them, which is something you do not have the power to do. Let others take responsibility for their own actions, and focus on how you can change yourself, which is something you can do. If you keep the "blame game" going, your family is likely to remain immersed in conflict, anger, and frustration.

Severe blaming also distorts your view of others. I've counseled parents who so blamed their child that they viewed the child as a "bad seed" or as a person who was simply "born to be bad." Sometimes a parent has a similar view of the child's other parent; for example, "His father is a rotten person." Your ability to search for solutions with other members of your family will be seriously compromised if you hang on to the irrational view that someone could be all bad. No human being is 100 percent bad!

A more helpful attitude to adopt is one of unconditional acceptance of yourself, your child's other parent, and your child as fallible human beings who will sometimes do things well and sometimes not so well (Ellis 1994). Also, rather than worry about who is to blame for your child's difficulties, try to focus more on how everyone in your family, especially you, can be part of the solution to helping your child function better.

4. *Fear of change*—Human beings have a great need for certainty and security. For this reason people sometimes prefer to hold on to the familiar, however unpleasant, rather than risk the uncertainty of change. If you find you are resisting or avoiding change in yourself or your family, ask yourself whether you might be fearful of change and why. If you can't answer this question, a consultation with a therapist might be helpful.

5. *Not following a child management plan long enough*—In my years of practice I have had many parents tell me they have tried every type of behavior modification technique with their child and "nothing works."

Upon closer examination of why these techniques failed, I often discover that the parents stopped using them after a few days. In fact, many of these so-called unhelpful techniques might actually have worked if the parents had used them consistently for a long enough period of time! I typically recommend that parents try the methods in this book consistently for 12 *weeks*. If at the end of a twelve-week period you see no response in your child, it might be worth a return to the drawing board to develop a new strategy.

During the twelve weeks that you are using the methods described in this book, you may see rapid behavioral improvement in your child that lasts. It is more likely, however, that your child will display an initial burst of good behavior that vanishes after a week or two and is replaced by a return of oppositional, defiant, and aggressive behavior. Do not get discouraged when this happens, and do not give up on the plan. The path to recovery for many children with disruptive behavior disorders is strewn with periods of difficult behavior that gradually yield to longer periods of cooperative behavior when parents hang in there long enough to get results.

CAUSES OF DEFIANT AND AGGRESSIVE BEHAVIOR IN CHILDREN

Another aspect of getting ready for environmental change involves developing some understanding of the causes of oppositional, defiant, and aggressive behavior in children. The following section outlines the major causes of these particular childhood problems.

1. *Failure to reward good behavior*—In families where problems have developed and a child is displaying oppositional/defiant/aggressive behavior, it is known that parents consistently fail to notice, praise, and reward (reinforce) the child's good behavior (Kazdin 1985, Lewis 1991). The child therefore has little reason to display good behavior since he knows his parents will not respond to it. It is also often the case in these families that parents angrily respond to the child's bad or inappropriate behavior. Thus oppositional, defiant, and aggressive behaviors become the means by which children gain some attention from their parents, even if it is negative attention. Figure 1–1 illustrates the negative attention syndrome.

2. *Failure to punish bad behavior appropriately*—Again, in families where serious problems have developed it is also known that parents fail to punish in appropriate ways the child's bad (inappropriate) behavior (Lewis 1991). Thus children in these families receive few rewards for good behavior and very little appropriate punishment for bad behavior. The stage is then set for the child to display a range of unchallenged oppositional and defiant behaviors that gradually become fixed aspects of the child's developing personality.

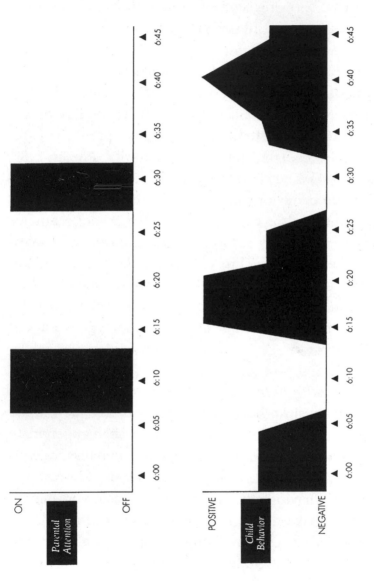

Figure 1–1. THE NEGATIVE ATTENTION SYNDROME

Adapted from *The Competence Approach to Parenting* by J. M. Strayhorn, copyright © 1995 by Strayhorn Publications. Used by permission of the author.

Investigators have also found that in some of these same families parents allow all kinds of misbehavior to go unchecked and then periodically crack down with excessively harsh or abusive punishment. Such inconsistent behavior by parents places defiant children at greater risk for full-blown antisocial behavior in adolescence and later life (Kazdin 1985).

3. *Excessive use of punishment*—Overreliance on punishment is an approach that creates many more problems than it solves. First of all, parents who use lots of punishment with their oppositional children often tell me that no punishment works, and they are absolutely right. Children who are under a barrage of parental punishment become immune to it because they have no way to escape such treatment. Also, whoever dishes out the most punishment in the family usually receives the most punishment from the child in return (Forehand and McMahon 1981). Furthermore, excessive use of punishment trains the child to lie and to engage in sneaky behavior to avoid punishment. In families where overreliance on punishment is the main child management strategy, children begin to feel fearful of their parents and may actively avoid them. Finally, although overreliance on punishment may stop oppositional behavior today, it does not change the child's behavior in the long run. It also does not change the child's motivation for misbehaving (Forehand and McMahon 1981).

4. *Failure to follow a plan consistently*—In some families parents alternate endlessly among starting, stopping, and changing their child management plan. Over time this lack of consistency can actually make the child's behavior problems worse. When you do not enforce the rules of your home consistently, your child learns that sometimes he can get away with things. In other words, his noncompliant behaviors receive "intermittent" or "periodic" reinforcement. Behaviors that are intermittently reinforced or rewarded ultimately become resistant to change. Each time you decide not to follow through with your rules, incentives, and penalties, you strengthen some of your child's oppositional behavior.

5. *Child temperament*—Studies show that children are born with different temperaments (Chess and Thomas 1991). Some are born friendly, outgoing, flexible, and cooperative. Others are more difficult, rigid, demanding, and aggressive. Your child's temperament plays a role in how he or she behaves and how well he or she follows your rules. If your boy or girl has a more "difficult" temperament, try to reinforce his strengths and any effort he makes to be cooperative. It is also important to remember that any child, however difficult, is a unique individual with preferences, desires, ideas, and feelings that require parental attention and support.

6. *Stress on the child*—Although children often won't admit it, they are quite vulnerable to stress. Common stres-

sors for children include chronic exposure to yelling in the home, long hours out of the home at school and day-care programs, chronic conflict with siblings, not having enough fun time with parents, having too many extra-curricular activities, or simply being hungry or tired. Under some or all of these conditions, many children become irritable and uncooperative. Try to identify the most visible stressors for your son or daughter and see if you can reduce the overall amount of stress in your child's life. By doing so you may see gradual improvement in mood and in his or her willingness to cooperate with the rules of the home.

7. *Stress on parents*—Stress on you can play an indirect role in perpetuating your child's behavior problems. When you are stressed out, you may be less likely to follow your chosen child management plan. When you let your plan slide, you intermittently reinforce your child's inappropriate behavior, which again strengthens the oppositional behaviors you would like your child to discard.

8. *The child's irrational attitudes and poor problem-solving skills*—Virtually all oppositional, defiant, and aggressive children display irrational (self-defeating) attitudes and poor problem-solving skills. In day-to-day situations these developing personality characteristics and skill deficits show up in the form of low frustration tolerance, demanding attitudes, aggressive behaviors, temper out-

bursts, impulsivity, poor verbal skills, and stubbornness. These symptoms reflect your child's self-defeating efforts to cope with frustration and to solve problems.

9. *Rewarding inappropriate behavior*—Many parents inadvertently do or say things that actually reward or reinforce a child's inappropriate or disruptive behavior. For example, parents sometimes laugh at the child's disobedient behavior or they stop talking and pay attention to the child who repeatedly interrupts their conversations with others. In other cases parents offer hugs and kisses to a child who is in the midst of a temper tantrum or they buy candy for the child who starts to fuss or cry in the supermarket.

In all of these situations the parental laughter, attention, or rewards strengthen the child's inappropriate behaviors. Disobedient behavior is also strengthened and rewarded when parents back off and do not follow through on directions given to the child simply because the child begins to whine, complain, or protest having to do something he or she does not want to do. In this type of situation the child learns that if he offers enough resistance or protest he can pretty much get his own way.

10. *The nagging, threatening, screaming/spanking syndrome*—This three-phase syndrome described by Patterson and colleagues (1975) and Barkley (1997) is common in families. The following description of each of these phases will show you how your nagging, threat-

ening, screaming, and spanking keep you and your child in conflict and teach your child to be oppositional.

The Nagging Phase

The nagging phase begins when you give a command to your child and he ignores or defies you. You then repeat your command, four times, five times, ten to fifteen times. Sometimes, just to get you off his back, your child does what he is told.

IMPACT OF THIS INTERACTION ON YOU—Even though nagging really doesn't train your child to cooperate, you keep nagging because sometimes it works a little bit. In other words, your child's occasional cooperative response to nagging intermittently reinforces your use of this unhelpful technique. Your child is training you to nag. What? Yes, your child is training you to nag!

IMPACT OF THIS INTERACTION ON YOUR CHILD—In those few seconds or minutes that your child is ignoring your nagging, he is learning that oppositional behavior pays off in two ways. The first payoff comes by avoiding a task that is probably not fun and requires effort, such as picking up toys or getting ready for bed. The second payoff comes in the form of buying a few more minutes of time with something that is fun, like watching television or playing with a toy. These two payoffs strengthen your child's oppositional behavior. Thus he or she continues to act in an oppositional manner when given a direction.

The Threatening Phase

Many times, oppositional children resist nagging completely. With mounting desperation parents then begin to threaten the child. The threatening phase begins when you again issue a command and threaten punishment if your child does not obey you. As long as your child ignores you or defies you, you continue to issue threats until you find the one that coerces him into doing what he was told or until you give up and walk away.

IMPACT OF THIS INTERACTION ON YOU—Like nagging, threats mostly do not teach children how to follow directions. But because threats work sometimes, you keep using them, sort of like the gambler who wins one bet out of a hundred and then endures another hundred losses for that one rare win. If and when you walk away from a confrontation with your child, you reinforce in yourself the unhelpful idea that you have no ability to influence your child to do better. When you think this way, it reflects that your child is training you to let him "do his own thing."

IMPACT OF THIS INTERACTION ON YOUR CHILD—During the time that your child is successfully ignoring your threats, he is again receiving the same double payoff for noncompliant/ oppositional behavior, even if in the end he does what he is told. Thus, in future situations, he will continue to resist directions in the hope that he can gain some additional fun time and avoid an unpleasant task for as long as possible.

The Screaming/Spanking Phase

When nagging and threatening do not work, parents often advance to screaming at the child or delivering a spanking to force the child to behave. The screaming/spanking phase begins when you again issue a command and your child ignores you or speaks disrespectfully to you. Out of frustration you angrily spank your child or scream at him; he may begin to cry and do what he was told or angrily fight back. You are now in a physical or verbal fight with your child!

IMPACT OF THIS INTERACTION ON YOU—At this point parents have generally lost control of their anger and are resorting to their superior physical strength to make the child follow directions or their superior mental strength to psychologically hurt the child for being so difficult. Again, because these unhelpful tactics sometimes work at the moment, even though they do not change the child's behavior in the long run, parents continue to use them. The price you pay, however, is guilt for the harm these methods do to your relationship with your child.

IMPACT OF THIS INTERACTION ON YOUR CHILD—Being verbally abused or spanked by a parent will likely result in the child's secretly being fearful of the parent and his/her anger control problem. Children treated in this way also tend to use yelling and hitting as a means of solving problems. Remember, children learn more from their parents' behavior than from their parents' words.

Parents and children caught up in this vicious cycle quickly realize that the winner is whoever escalates the fastest to using loud, angry, and coercive behavior. In other words, in those moments when you are overly stressed you may decide to skip nagging and threatening and go right to spanking or screaming. Or if your child is stressed or tired, he may decide to abandon ignoring you and stage a royal temper tantrum to get you to back off. Do what you can to prevent problems with your child from escalating in this unhelpful way. Remember, you need to take the lead as a role model for your child by demonstrating emotional and behavioral control when you and your child are in conflict.

You may now be wondering, "How do I break this cycle?" We'll get to that in Chapter 4. I will tell you at this point, however, that the way to end this dysfunctional interaction is to train your child to respond to your first command within ten to fifteen seconds—yes, ten to fifteen seconds! Now let's move on to review several specific learning theory principles that will help you better utilize the techniques in this book.

FOUR SOCIAL LEARNING PRINCIPLES

Studies show that parents who have some familiarity with social learning theory are better able to learn and master the techniques required to help oppositional children function more appropriately (Forehand and McMahon

1981). Below are four key social learning principles you should know to help you with your child management plan. They are based in part on Forehand and McMahon's (1981) review of social learning theory.

1. *Most behavior is learned*—People generally learn behavior patterns from others. To teach your child new behaviors, provide specific verbal prompts for desired behaviors and immediate verbal feedback. Model the specific behaviors you want your child to display and provide positive consequences for good behavior and negative consequences for bad behavior.

2. *Most behavior can be changed by the consequences of the behavior*—The consequences that parents provide either strengthen or weaken specific behaviors displayed by the child. To strengthen your child's appropriate behaviors, reward them. To weaken his inappropriate behaviors, ignore them or provide appropriate penalties.

3. *Positive reinforcement for good behavior should preferably be used more often than punishment for bad behavior*—Positive social reinforcers such as praise and enthusiastic attention are critical for helping children learn appropriate behavioral and attitudinal skills. Praise good behavior immediately after the child has displayed good behavior. To help a child learn a new behavior, provide positive social reinforcement every time the child displays the desired behavior. Provide praise intermittently to help a child maintain a specific behavioral skill.

4. *Punishment for bad behavior should preferably be used sparingly*—Punishments such as "time-out" help to eliminate oppositional, defiant, and aggressive behavior in children. For punishment to be effective it should be used as little as possible; occur immediately after the child displays the unwanted behavior; be carried out in the same manner each time it is used; be handled in a calm, businesslike way; and be of short duration.

This chapter has covered a variety of issues designed to help you begin to create a recovery-oriented home environment for your oppositional, defiant, and aggressive child. Assuming that all systems are "go," let's now move on to Part 2 of "Getting Ready for Change"—reviewing and, if necessary, changing your parenting attitudes.

KEY POINTS TO REMEMBER

1. Do not rush through this book. Give yourself time to contemplate, think through, and master the material in this and all subsequent chapters.
2. Persistent oppositional, defiant, and aggressive behavior places your child at risk for much more serious problems in adolescence and later life.
3. You are in control of many factors that either create or eliminate oppositional, defiant, and aggressive behavior in your child.

4. Instead of blaming others, focus on how you can be part of the solution to your child's problems.

5. Every day ask yourself whether you are creating and maintaining a recovery-oriented home environment for your defiant child.

6. Yelling, screaming, nagging, and threatening will make your child's problems worse. I have yet to meet the child who has been "screamed" into being a permanently cooperative citizen.

7. Keep the interventions described in this book going for at least three months.

8. Always maintain a sense of optimism about your child's ability to show more self-control and better behavior.

9. Review the section on social learning principles one more time before you move on to the next chapter.

2

Are Your Parenting Attitudes Helpful or Harmful?

The parenting attitudes you adopt will either help or hinder your efforts to help your child. The goal of this chapter is to help you develop rational parenting attitudes that will increase the chances that you will be able to help your oppositional child function better; improve the emotional atmosphere of your home; give you several psychological tolls to cope with your child's behavior problems; and prevent you from over- or underreacting to your child's defiance and aggression.

All human beings have ideas and attitudes about themselves, others, and the world. Some of the ideas we hold are rational (helpful); some are irrational (unhelpful). Rational ideas are ideas that can be supported by evidence; are flexible; fit with how the world works; generally, but not always, help you achieve your goals; and lead to moderate, appropriate displays of emotion and behavior (e.g., sadness, frustration, disappointment, mild anger) (Ellis and Dryden 1987). Irrational ideas are ideas that cannot be supported by evidence; are rigid and absolutistic; do not fit with how the world works; frequently prevent you from achieving your goals in life; and lead to disturbed, inappropriate displays of emotion and behavior (e.g., rage, deep depression, panic) (Ellis and Dryden 1987). As is the case for most parents, your approach to parenting is probably based on a combination of rational and irrational ideas about your child and his defiant behavior. Use this chapter to self-diagnose any unhelpful ideas you may have about your child and his disruptive behavior and to strengthen rational parenting attitudes and ideas. Also, as you review this chapter, keep the following key point in mind: *your oppositional/defiant child does not make you enraged, depressed, or panicked.* You enrage, depress, or panic yourself based on the way you think about or evaluate your child's behavioral difficulties.

The rational parenting attitudes to strive for occupy the middle ground of four lines of thought commonly found in individuals and families (Ellis 1975, Huber and Baruth 1989). These lines of thought are (1) Demandingness–Preferential Thinking–Not Caring; (2) Feeling Crushed–Feeling Concern–Seeing/Feeling Nothing; (3) Frustration Intolerance–Frustration Tolerance–Frustration Denial; (4) "Trashing" Others–Acceptance of Others–Worshiping Others. The beginning and the end of each of these attitude continuums are extreme and irrational and will reduce your chances of helping your child learn new behaviors and attitudes (see Table 2–1). Read on, identify, tear up, and discard your irrational attitudes toward your child and his/her disobedient behavior.

RATIONAL AND IRRATIONAL PARENTING ATTITUDES

1. *Demandingness–Preferential Thinking–Not Caring—Demandingness* is an attitude or state of mind in which a parent, in godlike fashion, thinks, "My children and

TABLE 2–1. Rational and Irrational Parenting Attitudes

1. Demandingness irrational	Preferential Thinking rational	Not Caring irrational
2. Feeling Crushed irrational	Feeling Concern rational	Seeing/Feeling Nothing rational
3. Frustration Intolerance irrational	Frustration Tolerance rational	Frustration Denial irrational
4. "Trashing" Others irrational	Acceptance of Others rational	Worshiping Others irrational

Adapted from *Rational-Emotive Family Therapy: A Systems Perspective* by C. Huber and L. Baruth, copyright © 1989 by Springer Publishing Co., New York, NY 10012. Used by permission of the publisher.

others must behave the way that I decree." This type of thinking is rigid, grandiose, arrogant, and irrational, because there is no law of the universe that says that anyone, even your children, must or should behave in the way you demand. Demandingness does nothing more than set you up to be angry because, as you already know, your oppositional child will at times break your self-proclaimed laws. The psychological mechanism that leads to a "demanding" point of view is your tendency to transform your legitimate preferences and desires into rigid, intolerant, absolute demands. You tell yourself, "Because I want my child to show better behavior, he absolutely must do what I say." This is not a logical conclusion because, again, there is no law of the universe that says your child must, should, or ought to behave, though it would be highly preferable if he did.

At the other end of this line of thought is the attitude of not caring about your child and his or her oppositional behavior. Parents sometimes express this attitude by ignoring the child's troubles and dropping all expectations. At this point parental thinking is something like, "My child is a hopeless case. I don't have the strength to care anymore. He can just do whatever he wants." The switch to not caring usually occurs after some intense, unsuccessful period of demandingness. In other words, when it becomes clear to parents that demandingness does not work, they will sometimes resort to washing their hands of the whole matter of trying to help an oppositional/ defiant child learn new behavioral skills. Now let me ask: How is not caring going to help you achieve your goals for your child? Where is the evidence that not caring helps children function better?

The rational attitude to develop and maintain is one that consistently focuses on your strong preference for your child to cooperate and obey your rules. Tell yourself, "I hope that my child will learn to cooperate, and I will stay involved as long as necessary to teach, guide, and influence him to do better, but he never has to." This type of thinking will reduce your anger and lead to more moderate feelings of concern and frustration when your child misbehaves.

Parents often misunderstand what I am talking about when I suggest that they give up their demanding attitudes toward their oppositional children. Many parents think I am encouraging them to be soft or wishy-washy on misbehavior, which is not at all what I mean. What I am talking about is a way for parents to have more emotional control when the child *is* disobedient, while at the same time setting firm limits on misbehavior and delivering penalties swiftly and decisively.

2. *Feeling Crushed–Feeling Concern–Seeing/Feeling Nothing*—Feeling crushed or devastated is the state of mind in which a parent thinks: "It's horrible, terrible, and awful that my child is acting this way. I'm totally crushed by his or her catastrophically bad behavior." This type of thinking is irrational, because the words *horrible*, *terrible*, and *awful* mean that something is 110 percent bad—worse than the worst thing that could ever happen to a person (Ellis and Dryden 1987). Now, let me ask: Is your child's bad behavior really horrible? Is it even the worst thing that could ever happen to you, like having your house burn down or having your whole family die in a plane crash? To give up your "devastation" thinking, create a personal catastrophe scale that will help you put your child's behavior problems in a more realistic perspective (see Table 2–2). Also, stop using the words *horrible*, *awful*, and *terrible*. Instead, substitute the word *unfortunate*. It's *unfortunate* when your oppositional child does not behave well, but hardly a horrible catastrophe.

At the other end of this line of thinking is seeing/feeling nothing (SFN). SFN, or *denial*, refers to a conscious or unconscious decision to block out or not notice some-

TABLE 2–2. Personal Catastrophe Scale

---

10 = Horrible–Terrible–Awful = worse than the worst thing that could ever happen to me

9 to 1 = Unfortunate events or circumstances

Horrible	→	10 -An atom bomb destroys my state—everyone dies.
The worst	→	9 - My whole family dies.
		8 - A car accident leaves me paralyzed.
		7 - My spouse divorces me.
		6 - My house burns down.
		5 - I lose my job.
		4 - My child is oppositional and defiant.
		3 - My car is stolen.
		2 - I bounce a check.
		1 - I lose my comb.

---

thing that does exist. SFN expresses itself through statements such as, "We have no problems in our family," "Absolutely nothing is wrong with me or my child," "We all feel fine," "Boys will be boys," and so on. SFN (denial) and its close friend *minimization*, the tendency to greatly downplay a problem, easily allow parents to escape and avoid the hard work of helping an oppositional child. In the long run, however, a denial state of mind will place your child at greater risk, because you are not letting yourself see his problem or possible solutions. In the meantime your child's bad behavioral habits are getting worse.

The rational ground between these extreme frames of reference is to acknowledge and admit that your defiant child has a problem and allow yourself to feel disappointment and concern rather than devastation or denial. Your disappointment and concern can be used to propel you toward creative solutions to your child's problems.

3. *Frustration Intolerance–Frustration Tolerance–Frustration Denial*—Frustration *in*tolerance means that you often give up when things are hard. Frustration intolerance is expressed when a parent thinks: "I must get cooperation from my child easily and without effort, because I can't stand the physical and mental discomfort I feel when things are hard. My child should just know how to behave better on his own." This attitude leads to inconsistency in parenting because some parents irrationally believe that they should not have to work and sweat and "hang in there" to get results and, further, that working hard and tolerating discomfort would in some way be life threatening. It should be obvious that this type of thinking will prevent you from following through on this or any other plan to help your oppositional child. Effective parents frequently tolerate discomfort and frustration to create consistency in their approaches to problem solving with their children.

At the other extreme is frustration denial. Frustration denial is a defensive attitude used by some parents to ward off awareness of how much they actually fear or dread frustration and discomfort. Frustration denial is present when a parent thinks: "Because I don't want to notice how much I can't stand frustration and discomfort, I'll pretend that nothing bothers me. Yes, that's right, *noth-*

ing bothers me." At best, this type of false self-assurance produces superficial or half-hearted support for your child management plan because your underlying dread of discomfort is still present and influencing your behavior. To challenge your attempt not to notice your fear of discomfort, ask yourself: "Is it true that nothing bothers me? Do I really handle frustration and discomfort so well?" To challenge your core fear of discomfort, ask yourself: "Where is the evidence that I can't stand discomfort? Has frustration or discomfort ever killed anyone?" By shedding your frustration denial and tearing up your fear of discomfort, you will be better able to tolerate the very real discomfort and frustration you will at times experience in parenting an oppositional child.

The rational attitude to adopt is frustration tolerance. Genuine frustration tolerance will help you be consistent, prevent you from overreacting or giving up on your child, and allow you to withstand—with discomfort—displays of defiance, disobedience, and disrespect from your child. To develop frustration tolerance, tell yourself: "Parenting an oppositional child is hard and frustrating but not too hard, and I can handle it. Without hard work and effort every day I will probably not achieve my goal of helping my child develop better behavioral habits. I really dislike it when my child is disobedient and disrespectful, but I'm not going to give up on my plan to help him."

4. *"Trashing" Others–Acceptance of Others–Worshiping Others*—Trashing others is the tendency to totally and

globally put someone down or evaluate someone or your child as totally bad—100 percent bad. Trashing is based on the mistaken notion that you can judge another human being's worth as a person on the basis of his behavior. Trashing beliefs toward children usually takes the form: "Because you disobeyed me, you are a totally bad child who deserves to be severely punished." To avoid this extreme attitude, you need to challenge and throw out the unhelpful idea that a child's worth is determined by his or her behavior. It is appropriate to rate your child's behavior as good or bad, but his worth as a person is never in question. Also, for a person to be judged as totally bad he or she would have to behave badly 100 percent of the time, which is never the case, even for a criminal on death row.

It is equally irrational to increase the worth of another person or your child based on good behavior. This tendency is known as worshiping others, and it is expressed in thoughts like: "Because my child has done good deeds today and has restrained himself from acting badly, he is virtually a saint and really worthwhile as a person," or "My child's good behavior proves that he is a little angel, and his worth as a person is therefore elevated to near godlike proportions." Worshiping others means you are still rating the worth of others on the basis of their behavior.

The rational alternative to these irrational extremes is to develop and maintain an attitude of unconditional acceptance of yourself as a parent and of your oppositional child. All human beings are equally worthwhile and all human beings, including your oppositional/defiant child, are fallible. We sometimes succeed and sometimes fail, but our worth remains constant. Saints and criminals have the same value as human beings, though saints clearly behave better than criminals.

This chapter offers a philosophy of parenting that will prevent you from over- or underreacting to your child's disobedience. Overall, the optimal attitude toward the behaviorally troubled child is one in which parents consistently communicate their strong desire for their child to do well; use their frustration and disappointment to stimulate further problem solving; tolerate uncomfortable feelings and sensations that go with parenting, particularly when setting limits for the child; and communicate unconditional acceptance of the child. Several other attitudes will further increase the chances that your child will respond to the approach described in this book. Specifically, they are feelings of kindness toward the child, the capacity to provide limits and penalties in a firm yet loving way, and the capacity to forgive an oppositional child for being difficult.

COPING STATEMENTS FOR PARENTS OF OPPOSITIONAL CHILDREN

Practice the following coping statements frequently to support and sustain a rational parenting philosophy.

1. *To promote a "preferring" or "desiring" state of mind*: (a) "I very much prefer and hope that my child will learn to cooperate, but there is no law of the universe that says he ever has to." (b) "I am strong enough to remain in control while I communicate my preferences and expectations to my oppositional child." (c) "If I am getting overly angry, it means I am transforming my preferences into godlike demands for good behavior from my child." (d) "I can remain calm and still deliver penalties swiftly and decisively."

2. *To promote feelings of concern about the oppositional child's behavior*: (a) "It's unfortunate that my child is misbehaving, but hardly a catastrophe." (b) "Dealing with my child's oppositional and defiant behavior is not the worst thing that could happen to me." (c) "I can use my disappointment, frustration, and concern about my child's misbehavior to help me search for solutions."

3. *To promote frustration tolerance*: (a) "Although I would like parenting to be easy, it mostly is not an easy job." (b) "I will not get results from my chosen child management plan unless I persist through the hard times and tolerate many uncomfortable feelings." (c) "I can stand it when I feel uncomfortable or when I have to exert myself to make my plan for my child work." (d) "Though I do not like it, I can handle it when my child is disobedient or disrespectful."

4. *To promote acceptance of the oppositional/defiant child*: (a) "My oppositional child is always a worthwhile person though I may not like his behavior." (b) "All human beings, including children, are fallible. We sometimes do things well, but often make mistakes." (c) "I can forgive my oppositional child for being difficult." (d) "Even if my child never gets better I can still choose to accept him and find things in our relationship to enjoy."

KEY POINTS TO REMEMBER

1. When you think in a demanding way about your child's disobedience and choose an attitude of low frustration tolerance, you are more likely to overreact with yelling and screaming tactics or to underreact by giving up and acting as if you don't care or have no ability to influence your child's behavior.

2. When you think in a strongly preferential way about your child's bad behavior and choose an attitude of high frustration tolerance, you are more likely to handle the misbehavior in a swift, decisive, businesslike manner.

3. Always display kindness and compassion toward your child and unconditional acceptance of his or her worth as a person.

3

Positive Reinforcement Techniques

A nonviolent, praise-oriented home environment motivates the oppositional/defiant child to display better attitudes and behaviors. The goal of this chapter is to provide you with a range of easy-to-use techniques to promote cooperative, prosocial, nonviolent behavior in your child. The techniques in this chapter are described under three headings: shaping the tone of the home environment, positive social reinforcement, and privileges and rewards.

SHAPING THE EMOTIONAL, BEHAVIORAL, AND MORAL TONE OF THE HOME ENVIRONMENT

Remember, as the parent you are responsible for establishing and maintaining the emotional and behavioral tone of your home. Some homes have an overall tone of anger, hostility, and unending, unresolved conflict. Other homes have a sad, unhappy, depressive atmosphere. Still others have an overly fearful, anxious tone and a pervasive sense that the outside world is unsafe. In homes such as these, angry, unhappy, or fearful parents may not be able to fully respond to the child's emotional need for security or to fully and wholeheartedly work with a behaviorally troubled child to help him recover from his behavioral problem. Also, children may themselves become so angry, unhappy, or fearful that they are not able to learn new behaviors and attitudes.

The optimal home atmosphere to strive for is non-violent, relatively structured, upbeat or positive, praise oriented, and rich in incentives for good behavior. In shaping the tone of your home, you want to communicate to your children that you and your spouse are in charge of the home and that you are serious about children following rules and directions. It is also important to be clear about your rules and expectations. Below are eleven guidelines you can use to create a more positive atmosphere in your home.

1. *Be a role model.* I discussed this in Chapter 1, but it is so important it is worth mentioning again. It is critical that you model the behaviors and attitudes you want your child to learn. As much as you can, demonstrate cooperation, kindness, impulse control, high frustration tolerance, patience, playfulness, and nonaggressive ways to solve problems. This will greatly contribute to a more positive home atmosphere and will set a powerful example for your child to follow.

2. *Post the rules of the home.* The simple technique of posting your expectations and rules eliminates the possibility that your oppositional child may not know what your rules and expectations are. By writing down daily chores and tasks and posting them, you also reduce your child's sense that you are an arbitrary "dictator" who

sometimes makes pronouncements about the rules and at other times ignores them (see Table 3–1).

3. *Phrase directions as statements, not questions.* It is common for parents to tell children to do tasks with questions. For example, many parents would say, "James, would you go clean your bedroom now?" James's response might well be: "Well, now that you mention it, *no!*" Telling your child to do a chore with a question implies he has a choice, when in fact you have no intention of making certain tasks optional. Deliver your directions to your child in command form with a businesslike tone of voice. Reduce all other distractions such as television, and establish eye contact when you are giving directions. If necessary, have your child repeat your di-

TABLE 3–1. The Rules of Our Home

Daily Tasks	Do Behaviors	Don't Behaviors
1. Out of bed by 7:00 A.M.	1. Talk nicely to others	1. No talking back
2. Dressed, face washed, book bag ready by 7:30 A.M.	2. Follow directions	2. No hitting or cruelty
3. Homework done by 4:30 P.M.	3. Tell the truth	3. No lying
4. Clear table after dinner	4. Share toys with friends	4. No bossiness with friends
5. Shower by 7:00 P.M.	5. Be gentle with others	5. No door slamming
6. Bedtime by 8:30 P.M.	6. Be kind to the cat	
	7. Do chores before fun activities	
	8. Let Mom or Dad know if you're upset, worried, or angry, so that we can talk it out.	

rections. Using good "direction technique" conveys to the child that you are serious about what you want him to do. Knowing that parents mean business helps oppositional children to become more cooperative.

4. *Within reason, offer your child some choices.* Many oppositional children have a heightened need for control. To encourage greater cooperation and to reduce some areas of conflict between you and your child, it is at times reasonable and appropriate to offer your child a choice when a task needs to be done. For example, you might offer your child a choice to brush teeth now or in fifteen minutes, or to pick up toys before or after dinner, and so forth. The technique of offering reasonable choices allows you to demonstrate flexibility with your child and gives your child some sense of control over his or her life. If your child does not follow through on a choice or promise that he made, you then need to deal decisively with the oppositional behavior. The method for dealing with disobedience is described in the next chapter.

5. *Resolve conflicts privately with your spouse or partner.* It is generally advisable to work out your child management disagreements privately with your spouse or partner. In this way both of you can present yourselves to the children as a unified coparenting team. Open and heated parental disagreements often result in the child's seeing one parent as "the bad guy" and the other as "the good guy." This type of split is not helpful for either the

parents or the child. Except in abusive situations, you should publicly support your spouse or partner's judgment when he or she is in conflict with your child, even if you privately disagree. If you disagree with what your spouse is doing at a given point, talk it over later when the problem is behind you. Then work out a plan for handling the problem differently the next time it occurs.

6. *Eliminate all television shows and video games that display violent acts.* We now know that children who are prone to acting aggressively can be stimulated to display aggression following exposure to brutal scenes on television. Watching violence and aggression on television probably leads oppositional, defiant, aggressive children to imitate what they have seen on television, to believe the world is a violence-ridden place, and to believe they are justified in acting violently because they see others acting that way on television (King and Noshpitz 1991). It is estimated that during the course of growing up the average child sees 18,000 murders on television (Forehand and Long 1996).

Unfortunately, many of the television shows currently produced for consumption by children are filled with acts of violence and brutality. In recent years some of the most popular children's shows have been "Mighty Morphin Power Rangers," "Biker Mice from Mars," "Skysurfer Strike Force," "Beast Wars," "SWAT Kats: The Radical Squadron," "Road Runner" cartoons, "Street Sharks," "Fantastic Four," and "Superhuman Samurai Syber-Squad." Characters in these shows largely have no impulse control, no frustration tolerance, and no ability to solve problems nonviolently. Across the board these characters slam, crush, blast, flatten, shatter, and explode each other time and time again. Viewing such scenes for hours on end may deepen a violent or aggressive problem-solving "groove" in your child's mind. It may also make your child insensitive to the rights and feelings of other people.

I recommend that you eliminate all such shows from your child's daily television diet. Part of the remedy for childhood aggression is elimination of aggressive models, massive exposure to nonviolent models, and a clear signal from parents that nonviolent methods of problem solving are valued. If your child protests your decision to eliminate violent TV shows, tell him that until he consistently shows more concern, kindness, and respect for others, all such television shows will be banned.

7. *Actively introduce your child to books and videos that contain themes of kindness, cooperation, sharing, and caring about others.* Frequent exposure to nonviolent, prosocial models of human interaction may further help your child develop the necessary inner resources to display kindness, cooperation, and concern for others more frequently (Strayhorn 1988). Try to find some time each day to enjoy a prosocial story or video with your child. Your local librarian or bookstore/videostore owner or your child's teacher can help you search for appropriate stories to share with your child.

8. *Show respect and concern for your child's other parent.* Under all circumstances show respect and concern for your child's other parent. Criticizing, blaming, or insulting your child's other parent in your child's presence is like criticizing, blaming, or insulting half your child (Porter-Thal 1994). By showing respect to your child's other parent you will improve the atmosphere of your home, model tolerance and self-control for your child, and keep your child from being caught in the middle of parental crossfire.

When parents have divorced or separated, one or both individuals may become so bitter and angry that they vow to make life as miserable as possible for each other. A parent who remains angry and unforgiving toward a former spouse sets a poor example about how to deal with difficult life situations. Children are also often embarrassed and scared by their divorced parents' immature, playground-like squabbles and hostile exchanges of criticism. No matter how wronged you feel by your former spouse or partner, try to bury the hatchet. If you consistently show respect to your child's other parent, your child will love you for showing maturity and self-control. If your child's other parent continues to try to make your life miserable, don't go down to that level. Over time your child will know which parent is in control and which parent has a problem.

9. *Do not bring up yesterday's problems.* Yesterday is history. You can do nothing to change what has already

happened, so why bring it up? Dredging up past problems only makes others, including children, resentful.
Make each day a new opportunity for things to be better, and keep your sights on the future.

10. *Offer teachings in ethics and morality to your
child.* Many oppositional, defiant, and aggressive children
have serious gaps in the development of conscience. They
do not seem to care about what is right or wrong, show
little concern for the feelings of others, and experience
little or no remorse for acts of aggression or cruelty. It
is critical therefore that a significant amount of your
parenting focus on your child's moral development. You
can work on closing the gaps in your child's conscience
by looking for opportunities to talk about prosocial val-
ues, for example, honesty, truthfulness, kindness, compassion, and concern for others, or by encouraging appropriate displays of remorse for misbehavior and by
looking at day-to-day issues and problems in terms of
what is right, ethical, and moral, or wrong, unethical, and
immoral. You will also enhance the moral atmosphere
of your home if you take your child to church or temple
every week and also enroll him or her in religious instruc-
tion classes or church youth groups.

11. *Do no harm to your relationship with your defiant child.* It is critical that you not engage in behaviors or attitudes that will harm your relationship with
your child or that will lead your child to see you as

untrustworthy. The main relationship-damaging, trust-destroying parental behaviors are yelling, screaming, spanking, swearing, putdowns, shaming, and too much criticism. Behavior like this will push your child away from you and make it less likely that he or she will want to respond to your expectations and rules. Instead, constantly strive to engage in relationship- and trust-enhancing behaviors toward your child. Let your child know that you are always available to talk about problems, thoughts, and feelings, and that no matter how tough things get you will never reject him or her. Show love and approval through the use of kind words and attitudes of warmth and compassion and by way of hugs, kisses, and pats on the back. Let all of your interactions with your child be guided by the principle of trying to help your child overcome his or her problems and of doing no harm to the relationship.

POSITIVE SOCIAL REINFORCEMENT

Positive social reinforcement means that you pay enthusiastic attention to what your child is doing well or to any small steps your child takes toward a more cooperative attitude and more appropriate behaviors. All of the techniques in this section are forms of positive social reinforcement. To really help an oppositional/defiant child function better, you should plan to use all of the following techniques simultaneously.

Positive social reinforcement (praise) for specific prosocial behaviors—for example, cooperation, kindness, sharing, honesty—trains your child to display such behaviors more frequently. Since you have an endless supply of praise, you should be generous in dispensing it to your child. Over time your child will internalize your "praising voice" and begin to praise himself for displaying appropriate, cooperative behavior. For your praise to be most effective it should be aimed at specific behaviors and attitudes, delivered immediately and communicated with enthusiasm. When you praise your child, the tone of your voice is especially important. Be sure it has a clear, upward swing that communicates genuine pleasure and delight over your child's good behavior. The enthusiasm in your voice is a "melody" that children love to hear. Your praise will also be strengthened when combined with nonverbal signs of approval—a smile, a wink, a thumbs-up sign—and physical displays of warmth and approval, such as a hug, a pat on the back, or a gentle tousling of the hair.

Below are five ways in which you can give positive social reinforcement to your child each day. Provide such positive reinforcement in doses two to three times greater than the amount of punishment you deliver each day.

1. *Pay attention to your child's good behavior*—Over the course of a day increase your ability to notice what your child is doing well. If you believe you cannot find anything positive in your oppositional child's behavior,

you need to scan more closely for appropriate behavior. Research shows that children who are oppositional and defiant do not act this way all of the time (Barkley 1997). Even the most difficult children display some good behavior each day.

Examples:

"Jason, you're doing a very nice job of using your imagination and playing quietly right now."

"James, thank you for putting your dinner plate in the sink. That was helpful."

"Sara, I'm pleased that you started to brush your teeth as soon as I told you to. I like it when you follow directions. Good girl!"

"Susan, I really like how nicely you've been playing with your brother for the past few minutes."

2. *Compliance training periods*—This is a simple technique described by Barkley (1997). The technique stems from the idea that the oppositional/defiant child is relatively weak in the skill of being compliant or cooperative. Thus the child needs lots of "cooperation practice" to strengthen the skill of being cooperative. You can do compliance training in periods with your child once or twice a day; they're very easy to do. (You do not need to tell your child he is involved in a compliance training period.) The training technique is as follows: at some point during the day, call your child over to you and over the

course of five minutes give him two to four simple directions that require no effort. For example, when you are cooking dinner call your child into the kitchen and give several directions, such as, "Please hand me the salad dressing," "Get me a spoon," "Hand me the potholder." Each time your child responds to your command provide praise. If your child does not respond, wait a minute and then try a different simple command. If your child still does not respond, abandon the compliance training attempt and try again later. Again, compliance training provides your child with extra cooperation practice and exposes him to the social benefits of being cooperative; that is, he receives praise. This technique should be used until your child begins to display better cooperation skills.

Examples:

Dad is working on the car in the driveway. Tommy is playing in the front yard.

DAD: Tommy, come here for a minute.

TOMMY: What, Dad?

DAD: Hand me that yellow screwdriver.

Tommy goes to the toolbox, gets the screwdriver, and brings it to his father.

TOMMY: Here, Dad.

DAD: Thanks for your help, Tommy. I appreciate it when you follow directions.

Dad then creates two or three more simple tasks for Tommy to do, each time providing praise.

Mom is reading a book in the living room. Katie is coloring pictures in her bedroom.

MOM: Katie, come here please.

KATIE: What is it, Mom? I was coloring.

MOM: I know, but I'd like you to get me the bowl of potato chips from the dining room table.

Katie goes to the dining room, gets the bowl of chips, and brings it to her mother.

MOM: Thanks, sweetie. I appreciate it when you follow directions. Would you like a potato chip?

KATIE: Okay.

MOM: Katie, before you go back to coloring, please hand me that magazine on the table.

Katie goes to the table, gets the magazine, and hands it to Mom.

3. *The nightly review*—This is a wonderful technique developed by Strayhorn (1988). The technique involves spending a few minutes each evening reviewing with your child some of the positive things he or she has done that day. Specifically, the nightly review is a time for parents to celebrate with the child some progress he or she has

made that day in the areas of being cooperative, honest, patient, helpful, or kind to others. The review can be done at dinnertime, shortly before bedtime, or when you're tucking your child in for the night. The nightly review is a helpful way to deliver some additional positive reinforcement to your child.

Examples:

Dad is tucking Sarah in for the night.

DAD: Sarah, I was just remembering how you held the front door open for me this afternoon when I was bringing the groceries in from the car. That was very kind of you and helpful. This morning I also noticed that you shared some of your toys with your brother. I'm very proud of you for sharing.

Shortly before bedtime Mom talks to Kyle.

MOM: Kyle, you were really a good sport today when we had to cancel our trip to the park. You stayed calm and were able to find some other ways of having fun. Also, I really liked it when you told the truth about taking that quarter from your brother. Good job.

4. *Proudly discuss your child's progress with your spouse or partner*—This technique is an indirect way of providing positive social reinforcement to your child. Each day take a few minutes to proudly discuss with your

spouse or partner the progress your child has made that day. If you are a single parent, you may, as an alternative, get on the telephone and call Aunt Millie or a friend to convey your pleasure in your child's progress. Just be sure your child is within earshot when you use this technique. Children love to feel that their parents are boasting or bragging about them.

Examples:

Mom and Dad are talking in the living room and Jeff walks by.

MOM: Come here, Jeff, let me give you a hug.

Jeff goes to his mother and sits next to her on the sofa.

MOM turns to DAD: Jim, guess what Jeff did today? He got dressed this morning quickly without a fuss. This afternoon he fed the dog as soon as I asked him to. He's doing a great job of following directions today.

DAD says to MOM: Our boy is really trying hard to be more cooperative. That's terrific!

Dad and Susan are bringing groceries in from the market. Mom greets them at the front door.

DAD says to MOM: Laura, Susan was a real help at the store. She stayed close to me and didn't beg for treats. She also helped me push the shopping cart. I really enjoyed her company and her help.

MOM replies: I've also noticed that Susan is trying to be more helpful. This morning she helped me take out the trash. I'm really proud of her for showing such a cooperative attitude today.

5. *Spend twenty minutes per day with your child in a "special time" activity*—This technique described by Barkley (1997) is very important. It stems from the idea that by paying attention to your child's good play behavior, you will stir in your child a stronger desire to follow your rules and directions. In other words, it will help your child want to be more cooperative.

Initiate the special time activity by telling your child you would like to spend some time with him or her doing something fun. Let your child pick the activity, and then simply enjoy the activity. While playing with your child, be sure to praise his or her good play behavior. For example, if your child picked a coloring activity, you might comment on how well he is staying inside the borders of the figures on the page or what nice colors he has chosen to use. Whatever the activity is—arts and crafts, board games, fantasy play—comment frequently on your child's playfulness and good ideas during the play. If your child becomes disruptive or is not able to play by the rules, tell him that special time is over and that you and he will play again tomorrow. Provide seven "special times" for your child during the first week (one twenty-minute special time per day) and five special times per week thereafter indefinitely.

To appreciate the power of this technique, take a moment to think about the best boss you ever worked for. He or she probably was a person who had a good sense of humor, paid attention to your work, and was supportive, helpful, and attentive. I'd bet money that that boss stirred in you a desire to work hard and do a good job. The special time technique helps you treat your child like the best boss you ever had.

Examples:

Mom and Kyle are playing checkers.

MOM: Kyle, you really are thinking of some clever moves today. That's great.

Dad and Lisa are playing tag on the front lawn.

DAD: Lisa, you're such a fast runner I can hardly ever catch you. I'm impressed.

Dad and Daniel are looking at the pictures in a nature book.

DAD: Dan, I really like it that you like to learn about animals and insects. You're a smart guy with a good mind.

Mom and Susan are out on a walk and Susan has been pointing out squirrels and birds.

MOM: Susan, you really are good at spotting all the little creatures in our neighborhood. Let's see if we can spot some more.

PRIVILEGES AND REWARDS

Privileges should always be used as incentives to help an oppositional child display greater cooperation toward daily chores and self-care responsibilities. The technique is simple and contains the following two steps: (1) define all the activities your child enjoys each day as privileges—having a friend over, watching television, listening to music, bike riding, playing baseball, playing in the yard, or going to a friend's home; (2) allow use of these privileges only after your child has completed necessary chores and/or self-care tasks. The basic message to your child is, "You work before you play." Oppositional children usually begin to take daily responsibilities more seriously once it is clear that privileges are contingent upon satisfactory completion of work.

Material rewards can be used sparingly as incentives for cooperative behavior. Material rewards are inexpensive items such as baseball cards, stickers, candy treats, tiny toys, and comic books. Use material rewards in relation to specific chores or self-care responsibilities that your child finds especially difficult to accomplish. The prospect of some immediately available tangible reward usually helps to encourage cooperation from an oppositional child. As your child begins to display competence in a previously difficult area, provide lots of positive social reinforcement, that is, praise and enthusiastic attention, and gradually phase out the material rewards. For example, a child whose morning dressing routine has improved substantially in response to positive reinforcement, and a small "grab bag" toy each day, could be told that his toy would now be available on Fridays provided he gets dressed each school day without a hassle. After several weeks the tangible rewards can be stopped altogether and the new areas of competence maintained by positive social reinforcement alone.

Parents are sometimes reluctant to offer material rewards for cooperative behavior on the grounds that such an approach is a form of bribery, which it is not. Remember, bribery occurs when one person tries to entice another person to do something unethical or illegal. There is nothing unethical or illegal about trying to help an oppositional/defiant child learn better social, behavioral, and attitudinal skills. The incentives and rewards you offer to your child in exchange for his cooperative behavior are no different from the paychecks you receive from your employer for the hard work you give at the office.

As you prepare to use privileges and rewards to promote cooperation from your child, keep the following additional tips in mind: (1) tell your child the specific tasks and chores you expect him to start and complete each day; (2) explain the specific privileges and rewards he will gain through cooperative behavior and write them down on a chore/reward menu; (3) if your child does not earn a privilege or reward, he still has to complete the chore/task he was told to do before he is allowed to do anything else. Once the chore/task has been completed, he can then engage in play activities other than the ones listed on the chore/reward menu; and (4) if your child fails to earn a reward or privilege and he accuses you of taking away his privileges, calmly tell him that he took his privileges away from himself by choosing not to complete a specific task or set of tasks.

It is usually advisable to break the day into morning, afternoon, and evening routines. Start each segment of the day with a positive attitude. Communicate to your child that each part of the day is a new opportunity to display chore and task competence and cooperative attitudes and behaviors. Below is an example of how a typical chore/reward program might look for an 8-year-old oppositional child named Richard.

1. *Richard's morning routine*

Chores—Get up and make bed, wash up, get dressed, brush teeth, comb hair, get book bag ready. If Richard completes these tasks without a hassle by 7:30 A.M., he earns a reward before he goes to school. If a hassle occurs or tasks are not completed on time, no rewards are provided.

Possible rewards—Eat breakfast in front of the television while watching a nonviolent show, wear some "cool" sneakers or clothes to school, earn fifty cents' allowance, get a special snack treat in lunch bag, receive a small toy out of a grab bag, read a nonviolent comic book for a few minutes.

2. *Richard's afternoon routine*

Chores—Change into playclothes, do homework, empty the trash. If Richard completes all of these tasks by 3:45 P.M., he gets his privileges as a reward. If tasks are not done on time or if there is a hassle, rewards and privileges are not available.

Possible rewards (one or several may be used)—Play outside, have a friend over, watch half an hour of non-violent television, ride bike, play with nonviolent video games, go to a friend's house, go for a walk with Mom, do an arts and crafts activity.

3. *Richard's evening routine*

Chores—Help clean up after dinner, feed dog, take bath, brush teeth, get into pajamas. If Richard completes all of these tasks by 7 P.M., he earns privileges and rewards. If tasks are not completed by 7 P.M., rewards are not given.

Possible rewards—Fifteen minutes of wrestling with dad, special snack, half an hour of nonviolent television, bedtime fifteen minutes later, extra bedtime story, play a card game with Mom.

The consistent use of these positive methods of influence should, over time, produce more cooperative behaviors and attitudes in your child. Some children, however, also require penalties to help them learn more appropriate behaviors. So let's move on to talk about penalties for noncompliance, defiance, and aggression.

KEY POINTS TO REMEMBER

1. You are responsible for the overall emotional, behavioral, and moral tone of your home. Work to keep your home upbeat, praise oriented, ethically and morally aware, and relatively structured.

2. Always show respect for your child's other parent even if you are angry at your spouse or ex-spouse.

3. The behaviors and attitudes that will damage your relationship with your child are yelling, screaming, spanking, swearing, putdowns, shaming, and too much criticism.

4. The behaviors and attitudes that will strengthen your relationship with your child include talking in a sincere and polite way, verbalizing love and approval, demonstrating kindness, compassion, tolerance, and patience, and touching your child in gentle and affectionate ways.

5. Structure your child's day so that all work, self-care tasks, chores, and homework are done before he or she is allowed access to fun activities.

4

Penalties for Noncompliance, Defiance, and Aggression

The skillful use of penalties for noncompliance, defiance, and aggression can significantly reduce such behaviors in the behaviorally troubled child. In this chapter you will learn how to deliver penalties effectively; several specific penalty techniques, including the ignoring and time-out procedures; and what to do if your child refuses to go to time-out or is unable to calm down while on time-out. The final sections of this chapter discuss additional penalty techniques to reduce morning and bedtime behavior problems.

Remember, noncompliant, defiant, and aggressive behavior in children may be learned behaviors; that is, some of your child's disruptive, noncompliant behaviors can be thought of as learned "bad habits." The good news is that learned bad behaviors can be suppressed or buried beneath newly learned good behaviors. A child management approach that consistently uses positive social reinforcement for appropriate behavior and penalties for inappropriate behavior stands a reasonable chance of helping an oppositional child acquire better behavioral habits.

PENALTY SKILLS GROUND RULES

To get started, there are several penalty ground rules you need to keep in mind to increase the chances that your

penalties will be effective. Carefully review each of the
following guidelines.

1. Do not try to use reason or logic when providing your child with a penalty. Trying to reason with your
child in the midst of a conflict is like saying to him or
her, "Before you agree to accept your penalty, please
let me convince you of how right I am that you need a
penalty." You do not need your child's permission to
give a time-out.

2. Do not display emotion when providing penalties.
As much as possible try to remain calm and businesslike
when implementing a penalty. If you become overly emotional, it will reinforce (reward) your child's disruptive/
oppositional behavior and may even lead him to believe
he is in some kind of strange, exciting game with you.

3. Tolerate the frustration and discomfort you will
likely experience when you see your child upset over his
penalty. Some parents irrationally believe that children
must never be frustrated or upset. Thus, when the child
begins to display distress, parents back off from following through on a penalty. Remember, both you and your
child will survive the distress each of you experiences
when a penalty technique is used.

4. Do not start to use any of the following penalty
techniques if you believe that an emotional reaction such

as guilt or anxiety may prevent you from following through with a penalty. If the thought of setting limits or delivering penalties to your child stirs emotions that could possibly interfere with your ability to set limits, tell yourself that "setting limits and following through on penalties is a form of love. My child will be relieved that I am setting limits." If you still feel reluctant to set limits for your child, consult a therapist to remove your emotional blocks to limit setting and the use of penalties. Then begin to use the penalty techniques in this chapter.

5. Before using the time-out procedure, select a very dull, boring place in your home to use as the time-out spot. Good places to use are hallways, laundry rooms, and corners. Whatever place you choose should be safe and free of any objects your child could use as toys or distractions while on time-out.

6. Remember, deliver penalties immediately, in a businesslike tone of voice, and in the same way every time. Also, use penalties consistently outside the home. Most of the following penalty techniques can be used in public—restaurants, church, stores, or when visiting the home of a friend.

7. Before you start to use the penalties described in this chapter, tell your child about the penalty plan. Describe how you will use the ignoring and time-out procedures and what will happen if he refuses to go to time-

out. Then implement the penalties. At the end of this
chapter I have provided an example of how to discuss
the penalty plan with your child.

I recommend five specific penalty techniques to decrease oppositional, defiant, and aggressive behavior in
children. These techniques may appear simple, but skill
is required to use them effectively. The techniques are:
ignoring, time-out, loss of privileges, loss of allowance,
and work chores.

THE IGNORING TECHNIQUE AND
DIFFERENTIAL ATTENTION

Ignoring is a powerful way to decrease misbehavior.
When using the ignoring technique, keep in mind the
social learning principle that behavior that does not receive attention tends to weaken or disappear. Ignoring
can be used for many low-level inappropriate behaviors
such as whining, hounding, not taking no for an answer,
yelling, swearing, and temper tantrums. Do not use the
ignoring technique for any behavior that is potentially
dangerous or when your child may be about to harm
someone or destroy property. The ignoring technique
should be used as long as the child is engaging in the
inappropriate behavior you are trying to eliminate (Forehand and McMahon 1981).

Keep in mind that when you first begin to use the ignoring technique, you may see an increase in the disruptive or inappropriate behaviors you are ignoring. This increase is commonly known as an "extinction burst" (Kazdin 1994). It reflects your child's efforts to coerce and torture you into giving him what he wants. Tough it out through this phase; usually the behavior you are ignoring will diminish after some period of time.

The ignoring technique has three components described by Forehand and McMahon (1981): (1) *no eye contact or nonverbal cues*—do not look at or gesture to your child; (2) *no verbal contact*—do not say anything, especially if your child demands to know why he is being ignored; (3) *no physical contact*—do not respond if your child tries to tug on you, hug you, or sit on your lap. If necessary, leave the room to stop your child from initiating physical contact. Once your child has stopped the inappropriate behavior you are ignoring, be sure to return quickly to the use of positive social reinforcement for good behavior.

The combined use of praise for good behavior and ignoring for many bad behaviors constitutes the child management technique of differential attention. Differential attention means that you will pay lots of attention to your child's competent, prosocial attitudes and behaviors and no attention to your child's incompetent attitudes and behaviors. It often takes a lot of mental strength for parents to use this technique effectively, especially in resisting the urge to yell or scream at the child for engaging in annoying, negative behaviors. Figure 4–1 illustrates the technique of differential attention.

THE TIME-OUT PROCEDURE

Time-out is really an extreme form of ignoring, used when the child's behavior is so unacceptable that removal from the social group is necessary. Time-out communicates a powerful message to the child. The message is: "Your behavior is now so unacceptable you need to be isolated to rethink and readjust your behavior." Time-out can be used to help a child improve at following directions, completing chores, following the house rules, and learning self-care skills. It can also be used to reduce testing, manipulation, defiance, and aggression. Time-out is the penalty technique that decisively ends the nagging, threatening, screaming syndrome I discussed in Chapter 1.

The following general guidelines described by Barkley (1997) apply to all of the time-out procedures discussed below. (1) Time-out should be limited to five minutes except for the 2- or 3-year-old child, in which case time-out should be limited to two or three minutes, respectively. (2) Once the five minutes has been served, your child must be quiet for thirty seconds to gain release from time-out. If at the end of five minutes your child is not able to meet the conditions of thirty seconds of quiet,

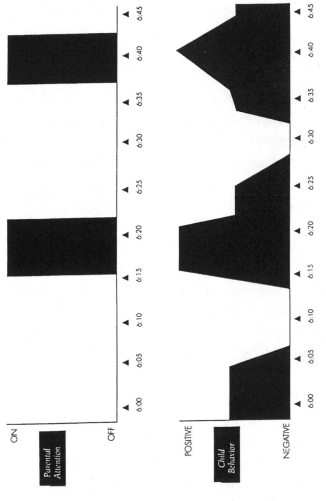

Figure 4-1. DIFFERENTIAL ATTENTION

Adapted from *The Competence Approach to Parenting* by J. M. Strayhorn, copyright © 1995 by Strayhorn Publications. Used by permission of the author.

time-out is extended for another few minutes until thirty seconds of quiet self-control is achieved. (3) Release from time-out is always a "contingent release." That is, before your child is released from time-out he must be quiet for thirty seconds and agree to do the task he was told to do in the first place or apologize for an act of aggression, property destruction, or disruptive behavior.

Once you tell your child to go to time-out, that's it! No second chances. Some children will try to manipulate their way out of time-out by scrambling to do the task they were told to do or by stopping an undesirable behavior and promising to be good. If this happens, tell your child, "Too late. Go to time-out now. You will do what you were told when time-out is over." Ignore any defiant talk that your child may direct at you while he heads for the time-out spot. Also, ignore your child if he tells you or acts as if he couldn't care less about your penalties. Believe me, your child cares. If your child reacts angrily, defiantly, or aggressively to the news that he has received a time-out, do not get into a punishment spiral of adding more and more punishments to the original five minutes of time-out. Remain calm and use your penalty skills to enforce the original time-out. If your child messes something on the way to time-out, he should clean up the mess after time-out and then do the task he was originally told to do. If, at the end of the time-out period, your child still refuses to do the task he was originally told to do or refuses to leave time-out, he immediately receives another time-out for not following directions and the entire procedure described below is repeated again and as many times as necessary to gain his cooperation.

1. *Time-out for not following directions*—The time-out procedure for use with a child who is not following directions is as follows: Give your child a clear command ("Jimmy, put your dirty clothes in the hamper"). Wait five seconds. If your child follows your direction, provide enthusiastic attention or praise immediately. If your child does not follow your direction, issue an incentive statement and a warning ("Jimmy, if you put your clothes in the hamper you will be able to go out to play. If you do not put your clothes in the hamper now you will receive a time-out"). Wait five more seconds. If your child does the desired task, provide enthusiastic attention or praise. If your child does not respond, send your child immediately to time-out ("Okay, Jimmy, you did not put your clothes in the hamper. Go to time-out now"). Figure 4–2 illustrates this time-out procedure.

2. *Time-out for not completing chores*—A variation of not following directions has to do with the child who will not complete chores. If your child has a chore to do, such as cleaning his bedroom or taking out the trash, estimate how long the job will take, set a kitchen timer for the estimated time, and tell your child that if the chore is not done by the time the timer rings he or she will be sent to time-out. If your child completes the chore be-

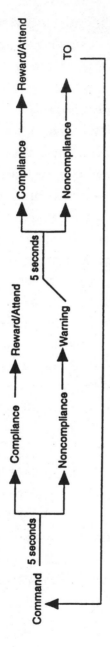

Figure 4–2. THE PARENTAL COMMAND–CONSEQUENCE PROCEDURE

From *Helping the Noncompliant Child* (p. 78) by R. L. Forehand and R. J. McMahon, copyright © 1981 by Guilford Publications. Used by permission of the publisher.

fore the timer rings, provide praise. If he does not, send him immediately to time-out (Barkley 1997).

3. *Time-out for hounding, badgering, interrupting, disrespectful talk, and not taking no for an answer*—Ignoring is often the best way to approach hounding, badgering, disrespectful talk, and not taking no for an answer. For some oppositional children, however, the use of time-out extinguishes such behaviors better than the ignoring technique.

The time-out technique for these unwanted behaviors is as follows: your child displays one of the above-mentioned behaviors. Tell him to stop the undesirable behavior he is displaying ("Steven, stop hounding me right now"). Wait five seconds. If your child stops the inappropriate behavior, praise him for showing self-control. If he persists with the undesirable behavior, issue an incentive statement and a warning ("Steven, if you stop your hounding you can still play. If you do not stop hounding me right now you will receive a time-out"). Wait five seconds. If your child stops, provide praise for showing self-control. If your child persists with the undesirable behavior, send him to time-out ("Okay, you did not stop hounding me. Go to time-out now"). Figure 4–2 also illustrates this form of time-out.

4. *Time-out for breaking posted rules of the home*—Time-out can also be used without a warning for any behavior that your child knows is a violation of the house

rules. Most parents forbid hitting, swearing, property destruction, disrespectful talk, stealing, lying, jumping on furniture, and cruelty toward people or animals. Once you review these rules with your child, post them, and explain that such behavior will result in an immediate time-out, he or she has been warned. No further warnings are necessary. If your child then breaks one of the posted rules, swiftly and decisively tell him to go to time-out. For example, Maryellen's son James has just verbalized a nasty four-letter word. She sternly says, "James, for swearing you now have a time-out. Go to the hallway now." Table 4–1 offers an example of how to post the rules for your child.

What to Do If Your Child Refuses to Go to Time-Out

Parents often wonder what to do if the child refuses to go to time-out. If your child has received a time-out and

TABLE 4–1. The Rules of Our Home

1. No hitting
2. No lying
3. No stealing
4. No jumping on furniture
5. No breaking things on purpose
6. No swearing
7. No talking back

If any of these rules are broken you will receive an immediate time-out. You have been warned.

ignores you, defiantly refuses to go, or goes but leaves the time-out spot before his time is up, you may pick one of three methods to deal decisively with this type of disobedience.

Method 1 for Refusal to Go to Time-Out

The simplest way to deal with a refusal to go or to stay in time-out is to prevent your child from engaging in any activities until the time-out has been served. Calmly tell your child, "You will not be allowed to watch television, use the computer, have snacks, play outside, or play in the game room until you do your five minutes of time-out." In using this method you need to be patient because initially it may take your child hours to agree to do the time-out. I recently read a case report in which it took a 5-year-old girl six hours to agree to do her five minutes of time-out (Windell 1994). After this initial confrontation with her parents the girl did her time-outs much more rapidly and her behavior began to improve.

If you choose to use this method there is one other aspect of the technique to keep in mind. Ignore your child while you are waiting for the time-out to be served. Do not talk to your child, argue with your child, or show that you are upset over the refusal to go to time-out. Go about your normal daily business, giving your child only the occasional reminder that once the time-out has been served and the original direction followed will he or she then be allowed to resume normal play activities.

Method 2 for Refusal to Go to Time-Out

A second method also prepares you to deal with refusals to go to time-out in a non-physical manner and has previously been described by Kavanagh and colleagues (1991). The technique is as follows. To the original five minutes add one extra minute of time-out for each refusal to go to time-out, up to a maximum of ten minutes. If your child still refuses to go after receiving ten minutes of time-out, tell him he now has a choice—either go to time-out for ten minutes or immediately lose an important privilege such as playing outside for two hours or losing television for two hours. If your child still refuses to go to time-out, remove the privilege and move on. I have found that for some children the loss of one privilege is not enough of a penalty to matter very much. If your child does not seem to care about the loss of one privilege, you may instead remove several important privileges for two hours when your child refuses to go to time-out (e.g., bike, TV, and playing outside).

When sent to time-out, some oppositional children refuse or are unable to calm themselves and persist in displaying loud, disruptive, and defiant behavior. If after fifteen minutes your child refuses to settle down and serve his minimum sentence of five to ten minutes, release him from the time-out attempt and instead remove one or several privileges for two hours (Kavanagh et al. 1991). When you do this, be sure to explain why you are changing the penalty: "John, since you are unable to accept a time-out now, you will instead not be able to ride your bike for the next two hours." Over time your child will probably learn that it is easier to take a five- or ten-minute time-out than to endure a two-hour privilege loss.

Method 3 for Refusal to Go to Time-Out

An alternate method for dealing with a refusal to go or stay in time-out has been described by Barkley (1997). This alternate method involves physical contact with your child and barrier restraint in his or her room if necessary. It is used in the following way. Your child is told to go to time-out but he refuses to go to the designated time-out spot or goes but leaves before his time-out is finished. A warning is then sternly issued that continued refusal to go to or stay in time-out will result in his being sent to his bed for the five-minute time-out. If your child continues to defy the time-out directive, calmly but firmly escort him to his bed and say that because of the refusal to take time-out in the usual space he must now complete time-out on the bed with the door to his room left open, provided he stays on the bed and in the room. Your child is then told that if he leaves the bed and the room before time-out is over, you will again place him in the bedroom, shut the door, and hold it or lock it shut if necessary. If your child leaves the room before the time-out period is over, he is immediately placed back in his room, with the door shut, for a minimum of five minutes and until he has calmed down and regained self-control. When locked in the bedroom, some defiant children will quiet and calm themselves quickly and be ready for release from time-out within a short period of time.

For other children, however, barrier restraint in the bedroom triggers an extended temper tantrum that includes yelling, hate speech, swearing, banging on the door, and property destruction. If this situation occurs, the child remains in the bedroom until he completes five minutes of time-out and then quiets himself for thirty seconds, even if it takes one to two hours to achieve thirty seconds of quiet. Once the first few major confrontations are over and your child understands that you absolutely will not respond to prolonged temper tantrums in the bedroom, it is very likely that he will work to achieve self-control more rapidly in order to gain release from time-out and from his room.

Before you decide to use this method of dealing with a refusal to go or stay in time-out, consider the following additional guidelines. If the bedroom is to be used for time-out either with the door open or closed, it should be stripped of all major toys or valuable items so that the child cannot have fun while on time-out or destroy valuable property when angry. Also, some mothers have a hard time of physically moving a child to the bedroom, and in trying to do so often find themselves in a chaotic and exhausting physical battle to get the child to his or her bedroom. This type of wild struggle is damaging to the parent–child relationship and also contains the potential for someone to get hurt. If this is your situation, I recommend that you only use one of the nonphysical methods for dealing with a refusal to go to time-out described in the previous sections.

What to Do If Your Child Refuses to Leave Time-Out

A child who refuses to leave time-out when told to do so is still not following directions. If your child refuses to leave time-out, simply tell him that he now has another five-minute time-out. Once the new five-minute time-out has been served, followed by thirty seconds of quiet, offer your child another opportunity to end the punishment and do what he or she was told to do in the first place. If your child again refuses to leave time-out, you repeat the time-out procedure again and do so as many times as is necessary to gain his cooperation (Forehand and Long 1996).

How to Talk to Your Child about the Penalty Plan

Before you begin to use differential attention, time-out, and loss of privileges, it is important that you meet with your child to review each step of the penalty plan. By doing so, your child will perceive you as fair, level-headed, and dead serious about the need for him or her to show improved behavior and attitudes. The following is an example of how to introduce your child to the use of penalties for disobedient behavior.

Margaret and John have just started a meeting at the kitchen table with their 8-year-old son, Zachary, who has displayed oppositional and defiant behavior for several years. Margaret begins the discussion.

"Zach, your father and I are very concerned about your general unwillingness to follow our directions and about your inability to take no for an answer when you want things you can't have or can't do. Starting this afternoon, Dad and I are going to make some changes in how we work with you when you disobey us. First of all, we are no longer going to nag you, yell at you, or scream or spank you. We don't think nagging, yelling, or screaming helps anybody learn to cooperate. Instead, we are going to use ignoring, time-out, and loss of privileges for your defiant or oppositional behavior. This is how it will work:

"For hounding, badgering, whining, and not taking no for an answer, we are going to ignore you until you stop such behavior even if it takes hours for you to stop. Once you stop these behaviors we will again talk to you and certainly let you know that we notice and appreciate your good behavior.

"When Dad or I give you a direction to do a chore or task or to stop certain bad behaviors, we will give you the direction one time only. If you ignore us or defy us, you will get one reminder about the benefits of cooperating and one warning that further refusal to do what you were told will result in your being sent to time-out on the stairs. If you go to time-out you will only need to sit for five minutes to get yourself together. After you serve five minutes of time-out you will need to be quiet for thirty seconds and then agree to do what you were told to do to gain release from time-out. If you refuse to go to time-out or leave time-out before your time is up, you will instead lose TV, the computer, and your bike for two hours. If you hit anyone or break property, you will be sent to time-out immediately, without a warning. Any questions?"

If Margaret and John had instead chosen the locked door technique for dealing with a refusal to go or stay in time-out, each stage of that method would need to be clearly explained to Zachary.

ALTERNATE PENALTY METHODS FOR DIFFICULT MORNING AND BEDTIME BEHAVIOR

Although it is perfectly reasonable to use time-out to deal with morning disobedience on school days or to deal with disruptive behavior at bedtime, there are alternate penalty methods that some parents find more practical to use at these specific times of the day. This section reviews the use of monetary fines and the use of work chores as alternate penalty strategies to improve morning and bedtime behavior. The following penalty techniques are for children 6 to 11 years of age.

Disruptive Morning Behavior

Mornings are pressured times for most families. Parents have to get themselves ready for work, make lunches for the children, keep the children on task with their routines, and attend to other chores such as taking care of pets and getting breakfast ready. Contrary to what parents want, many oppositional children do not function well in the morning and instead refuse to get out of bed or get dressed, or tease their siblings, or chase the family pet around the house, or engage in other disruptive behaviors. It is usually very hard for parents to try to manage and eliminate this type of behavior in the midst of all of the morning responsibilities. Thus, being human, parents often resort to nagging, yelling, and screaming to get the disobedient child moving in the morning. When the yelling starts the day begins on a sour note for everyone.

To end morning craziness and to help your child improve his or her functioning and behavior on school days, try the following incentive/penalty plan. On Monday mornings, place five one-dollar bills in a glass jar and put the jar on the kitchen counter where your child can see it easily. Tell your child that each morning that he or she cooperates and gets ready for school without a hassle, you will leave the money alone. If your child cooperates every morning of the week, he or she receives the entire five dollars on Friday afternoon as earned allowance. For each morning that your child is disobedient or creates a major hassle you calmly go to the jar and take back one dollar. In other words, you fine your child one dollar for each morning of disobedience or disruptive behavior. Whatever money is left at the end of the week is given to your child as his or her total allowance for the week. I have found that many defiant children, particularly 6- to 11-year-olds, will work to improve their behavior to get money and to prevent loss of money. I have had parents report dramatic improvement in their child's morning behavior using this technique.

If this method does not result in enough of an improvement in your child's behavior, you can add one other penalty consequence to the money plan. This involves the use of an after-school work chore for your child to do. It goes like this: take a glass jar and fill it with five or six pieces of paper, each of which has a fifteen-minute household chore written on it (e.g., vacuum the living room, rake leaves in the yard, dust the stairs and window-sills). Place the work chore jar on the kitchen counter next to the allowance jar. Show your child both jars, and say that for good behavior in the morning he or she will keep the money and not have to do a work chore later in the day. Bad behavior, however, will result in the loss of one dollar per day and the assignment of a work chore that will have to be done immediately after school and before the child is allowed to play. If homework is the first task to be done after school, the chore can be done immediately after the homework is completed, before access to fun activities is allowed. Although this work chore technique violates the basic principle of delivering penalties immediately, it does help some 6- to 11-year-old defiant children shape up in the morning since they strongly want to avoid work during prime afternoon playtime. When you use the work chore penalty techniques, be sure to explain to your child that his oppositional or disruptive behavior in the morning harms family life by creating stress for everyone. Thus the work chore is a symbolic act of restitution designed to help the family and make up for the harm done earlier in the day.

Disruptive Bedtime Behavior on School Nights

For many children with disruptive behavior disorders, bedtime is an especially difficult time of the day. Such children are often reluctant to go to bed, won't stay in bed, or get wild and create a huge disturbance just when everyone else wants to relax and unwind. Nighttime disobedience from children is often fueled by fears of being alone in a dark or semidark room or by other anxieties about not being safe when separated from parents at bedtime. To help your child display better behavior at bedtime, it is important that you make ongoing efforts to address and reduce your child's underlying nighttime anxieties. A consultation with a licensed child psychotherapist can help you to develop strategies to lower your child's overall level of bedtime worries. At a behavioral level, however, there are some incentive/penalty methods that you can use to help your child have greater self-control at bedtime.

The incentive/penalty technique to use at bedtime is the same earned allowance method used to improve morning behavior. Starting on Sunday evening, place five one-dollar bills in a jar and tell your child that for each school night that he gets ready for bed and gets to bed without a hassle, you will leave the money alone. If your child displays good bedtime behavior from Sunday through Thursday, the entire five dollars is given to him on Friday as earned allowance. For each evening that a hassle develops or disruptive behavior occurs, you take back as a fine one dollar. Whatever money is left at the end of the week is given to your child as allowance. I have also had parents report dramatic improvement in their child's bedtime behavior using this method.

If your child displays difficult behavior in the morning *and* at bedtime, you can use the earned/lost allowance method at both times of the day. If it looks like it might be too expensive to have your child earn a dollar in the morning and at bedtime for a total of ten dollars per week, you can go to the bank, get a roll of half dollars, and put ten half dollars in a jar on Sunday evening. Your child can then earn or lose fifty cents for each school night and for each school morning, depending on his or her behavior and level of cooperation. Using the half-dollar method allows the weekly total to remain at five dollars, which is a more reasonable amount for some parents to pay.

Before you use the work chore penalty method or the earned/lost allowance technique, consider the follow-

ing additional guidelines. First, it is important to remember that 4- and 5-year-old children are unlikely to respond
to these methods since children this young are often not
interested in money and will not work to avoid an unpleasant afternoon work chore. Young children are very
bound up in the activities of the present moment and are
not as oriented toward the immediate future as are some
6- to 11-year-old children. Thus the swift and decisive use
of time-out remains your best bet to improve morning
and bedtime behavior for 4- to 5-year-old children. Second, when using the work chore technique, be sure that
the chore is limited to fifteen minutes of work or less.
Remember, this punishment is designed to be a symbolic
act of restitution to the family and mildly aversive for the
child. Do not give your child excessively long or difficult
chores to do. Third, it is possible for the work chore technique to trigger a major burst of aggression and defiance
from your child, especially on days when he or she is in
good emotional control after school and for this reason
feels it is terribly unfair to be punished at a time when
things are going well. If after two weeks the work chore
technique results in no improvement in your child's
morning behavior and creates a royal afternoon battle
between you and your child, I recommend that you stop
using this method. Instead, go back to the swift and decisive use of time-out in the morning even if it means that
your child will be late for school.

Now that you have started to create a recovery-oriented home environment for your defiant child, it is time

to shift gears and team up with your child to help him or her develop better inner self-control skills. Let's move on.

KEY POINTS TO REMEMBER

1. Discuss all aspects of the penalty plan with your child before you begin to use the penalties described in this chapter.
2. Deliver penalties swiftly, decisively, and unemotionally.
3. Remember that setting limits and using appropriate penalties is a form of love.
4. Do not let your child manipulate or coerce you into not following through on an appropriate penalty.
5. Consult a therapist if you find that you are unable to set limits for your child or are unable to follow through on penalties.

5

Self-Control Skills
Part I: Building Thinking Skills

Behavior modification methods are effective in promoting better functioning in oppositional children. However, total reliance on external behavior modification techniques runs the risk of training your child to think his behavior can be controlled only by external forces. The goal of this chapter is to teach you the common forms of irrational thinking that contribute to your child's inappropriate behaviors and attitudes. This chapter will also provide you with a repertoire of rational, self-control–enhancing ideas you can teach your child to use when provoked, teased, challenged, or frustrated, and a way to encourage your child to be a flexible thinker. The more often your child can think flexibly and rationally about day-to-day problems and frustrations, the greater the chance he will display more appropriate behaviors, attitudes, and feelings. He may also begin to understand that his behavior can be controlled from within, by the process of using self-control–enhancing thoughts about social problems and frustrations.

TEACHING YOUR CHILD TO BE
A FLEXIBLE THINKER

Most defiant children are extremely rigid in their behavior patterns and attitudes. This psychological rigidity limits your child's problem-solving capacities, his ability to transition from one activity to another, and his ability to work at tasks cooperatively. It is important, therefore, that you encourage flexible thinking and behavior in your child.

To help your child develop flexible attitudes you first need to explain to him that one of his daily goals is to be a flexible thinker. Tell your child that flexible thinkers are strong people who have strong mental muscles that allow them to bend their thoughts in ways that keep them out of trouble. Let your child know that you believe he can be a strong, "thought-bending" flexible thinker if he works at it every day. Table 5–1 displays several common, rigid ideas or beliefs that contribute to your child's stubbornness and aggression and the flexible alternative

TABLE 5–1. Rigid vs. Flexible Attitudes

Rigid Attitudes	Mental Muscle	Flexible Attitudes
1. "I must get my way."	Bend	"I don't always have to get my way."
2. "I will not stop playing or doing what I want."	Bend	"I can 'shift gears' and do what Mom or Dad wants."
3. "I demand fairness all the time."	Bend	"I can handle unfairness."
4. "I must get revenge on others."	Bend	"I can forgive others."
5. "Yelling and hitting are the only ways to solve problems."	Bend	"There are many other better ways to solve problems."

ideas that will increase his ability to cooperate and to avoid trouble. Review these ideas with your child and encourage the idea of bending unhelpful, trouble-creating attitudes into helpful, trouble-avoiding attitudes. Flexible thinking is also required for your child to learn the rational self-control–enhancing beliefs and attitudes discussed in this chapter. As always, be ready to praise and reinforce any small steps your child takes toward flexible attitudes and behavior.

THE IRRATIONAL BELIEFS
OF DEFIANT CHILDREN

This section is based on the work of Albert Ellis (1994), the founder of rational-emotive behavior therapy (REBT), and Bernard and Joyce (1984), who have applied REBT principles to clinical work with children and adolescents. It covers the major irrational beliefs that cause your oppositional child's main behavioral problems, an analysis of why these beliefs are irrational, and the desired alternative rational beliefs that will help your child cope more adaptively and display better behaviors and attitudes.

Before you begin teaching your child rational thinking skills, a couple of points on teaching technique are in order. Teach your child to think rationally when he is calm, or gently offer a rational coping statement as a cue to your child when a problem is developing. When your child begins to use rational thinking to calm down or

control behavior, be sure to provide "enthusiastic attention" to his newly emerging thinking skills. If your child
has lost control and is very upset or angry, do not coach
him with rational thinking at that point because he may
develop resistance to rational thinking just to spite you.
Rather, wait until the storm has passed and then, as
needed, gently begin to reintroduce rational thinking. At
this stage it is also important to introduce your child to
the concept of "self-talk," that is, the private thoughts that
all people use to guide and shape attitudes and behavior
(Chapter 7 gives an example of a mother explaining the
idea of self-talk to her son). Tell your child that by incor-
porating some of the following rational coping statements
into his self-talk he or she will likely have more self-
control and be in trouble less often. A final point—it will
take much practice and repetition of the following ideas
to help your child develop greater self-control.

The material in this section is not an all-inclusive
review of the oppositional child's symptoms and irrational beliefs. It is, however, a look at some of the common
symptoms and irrational beliefs that oppositional/defiant
children display and use frequently. Carefully review the
following eight problem areas and the corresponding
"thinking remedies" so you can begin to teach your child
how to think flexibly and rationally. The sections on anger, cheating, lying, and stealing are brief summaries of
more extensive discussions of these problems by Bernard
and Joyce (1984). For the younger or very immature child

it will likely be necessary to offer shorter or more simplified versions of the rational alternative beliefs described below.

1. *Irrational beliefs associated with rage toward others*—Rageful anger occurs when your child rigidly believes: "Because I don't like what you are doing you must not do it." "Because you did that horrible act you are a total rat who deserves severe punishment." "You've got no right to treat me in this unfair way."

ANALYSIS—This type of thinking by your child is self-defeating because there is no law of the universe that says others must behave in the way your child demands; your child has irrationally rated another person's behavior as horrible—110 percent bad—worse than the worst thing that could ever happen to him, which it is not; your child has totally "trashed" another person as all bad, which is a distortion of reality; and your child is demanding that the world be fair when often it isn't.

RATIONAL ALTERNATIVE BELIEFS—To reduce rageful, hating, damning anger, teach your child to think: "I dislike your behavior but tough, that's the way you sometimes act." "It's a hassle that you treat me badly, but there are worse problems that could happen to a kid." "Like all kids you [the other kid] sometimes act badly but you are never an all bad person." "I wish the world was fair but many times it isn't. Tough! I can handle it."

2. *Irrational beliefs behind a defiant attitude toward adults*—A defiant attitude toward adults emerges when your child believes: "To feel worthwhile and powerful I must tell you off," and "By talking back to grown-ups I'll really prove that I rate as a person and have power."

ANALYSIS—Thinking like this is irrational because your child believes that his value as a person and his personal power are enhanced by acting in a provocative and defiant manner. He believes that self-worth is tied to behavior, good or bad, when logically it is not, and that personal power is evident only through a direct verbal assault on authority figures.

RATIONAL ALTERNATIVE BELIEFS—To reduce a defiant attitude, suggest the following ideas to your child: "I am always an okay, worthwhile kid, so I don't need to prove it by talking back," and "Words and ideas spoken in a nice tone of voice have power too."

3. *Irrational beliefs associated with oppositional behavior*—Oppositional behavior emerges when your child rigidly believes: "To prove that I am in control, I must resist directions and requests from grown-ups."

ANALYSIS—Although oppositional/noncompliant behavior is in many ways learned behavior, it often reflects the child's desire to demonstrate control over an adult. The irrational demand that your child places on him- or herself in this situation is a demand to resist at almost all costs. Also, your child irrationally believes that control is demonstrated only through resistance, when in fact control may be expressed in many other more adaptive ways.

RATIONAL ALTERNATIVE BELIEF—To help eliminate oppositional behavior, teach your child to think: "I am enough in control to show that I can cooperate and even do things I don't like to do."

4. *Irrational beliefs associated with lying*—Lying occurs when your child thinks: "To feel good about myself, I must behave perfectly." "If I mess up, I'm worthless and deserve punishment." "I cannot risk feeling worthless or getting punished, so I will lie about what I did."

ANALYSIS—Again, your child is irrationally linking self-worth to isolated behaviors and for this reason believes that lying will protect his fragile self-esteem. (Be aware, however, that lying is rational if a child has been receiving a great deal of harsh punishment. It is rational and self-protective to try to avoid severe punishment.)

RATIONAL ALTERNATIVE BELIEFS—To reduce lying, suggest the following ideas: "I messed up like all kids sometimes do, but I'm still okay and worthwhile as a person." "I'll admit that I acted badly, but I won't put myself down. Sometimes I make mistakes." "I am tough enough to tell the truth. If I do get punished, I can handle it."

5. *Irrational beliefs associated with cheating*—Cheating occurs when a child believes: "I am a *total* failure as a kid when I fail at something." "Failing is terrible. I can't handle the shame of not doing well, so I'll cheat to make myself look good."

ANALYSIS—This type of thinking is irrational. To be a total failure a child would have to fail continuously at everything from dawn to dusk, 365 days a year, which no child ever does. Failing at things, making mistakes, and not doing well, though unpleasant, are not horrible, terrible, and awful events. Failing at something is far from the worst thing that could ever happen to a child.

RATIONAL ALTERNATIVE BELIEFS—To help eliminate cheating, encourage the use of the following ideas: "Like all other kids, I will sometimes succeed and sometimes fail, but I am always worthwhile." "Although it's a hassle to fail and it feels unpleasant, there are worse things that could happen to me. I can handle it."

6. *Irrational beliefs associated with stealing*—Stealing occurs when your child believes: "I'm not getting the kind of approval that I demand, so I'm going to steal anything I want to make myself feel better." "I must always get my fair share of 'goodies' in this unfair world." "I can't stand it [i.e., I'll die] if others have more than I have."

ANALYSIS—This type of thinking is dysfunctional because your child wrongly believes that self-worth is improved by taking things, or that taking things is an adequate substitute for parental approval, when clearly it is not. He also believes the world must be fair even though often it is not, and that it is "horrible" not to have as much as others have.

RATIONAL ALTERNATIVE BELIEFS—To help your child stop stealing, promote the following ideas: "I am a worthwhile person whether or not I am getting approval and attention from others." "I'll likely never have as much as some people have. Tough! That's the way it is in this world." "I'll live if others have more than me and I can still have fun." "It's not that bad if others have more than I do."

7. *Irrational beliefs associated with low frustration tolerance*—Low frustration tolerance occurs when your child thinks: "I must always get what I want immediately and easily"; "Adults must never make me do things I don't want to do"; "It's horrible when I can't get what I want"; "I can't stand not getting what I want or getting what I don't want."

ANALYSIS—These beliefs are self-defeating because your child believes that rigid, demanding attitudes will make life easy, even though much of what we obtain or acquire in life requires effort and hard work. He also believes he has the godlike power to determine the workings of the world, even though frequently the world dishes out things we don't want but have to cope with nonetheless. He also feels it is a horror not to get what he wants immediately (when clearly it is not), and that death, fainting, or paralysis will occur if he does not get what he wants or if he gets something that he doesn't want.

RATIONAL ALTERNATIVE BELIEFS—To improve frustration tolerance, suggest the following ideas: "Although I would like to get what I want easily, I'm probably going to have to work hard and tolerate uncomfortable feelings to get what I want." "It's a pain that I can't get what I want or have to deal with things that I don't want, but it's not a disaster." "I can handle it when I can't get what I want," "I can handle it when I have to deal with something that I don't want. I'll live."

8. *Irrational beliefs associated with property destruction*—Property destruction and physical aggression may occur when your child believes: "My personal worth is destroyed if you mess with me in any way, so I will destroy you [you piece of trash] or your property to make you hurt real bad."

ANALYSIS—This is extremely irrational thinking because your child believes that his self-esteem depends on what another person says or does, when it does not. He also believes another person is all bad, which is not possible, that hateful, destructive revenge can restore self-worth or self-esteem, which it cannot, and that forgiveness toward others is not possible, when it is.

RATIONAL ALTERNATIVE BELIEFS—To reduce aggression toward others, offer the following ideas: "I am always worthwhile and okay, even when someone else gets in my way or treats me disrespectfully or unfairly." "There are no all-bad people, only people who sometimes act badly." "I am already a worthwhile kid, so I don't have to hurt others or their belongings to know that I am okay." "I can forgive people for treating me badly."

Encourage your child to use these coping statements frequently. As he begins to use these self-control–enhancing ideas when provoked, teased, or frustrated, he will be better able to modulate feelings and behavior, solve day-to-day problems, stay out of trouble, and have more fun. And be sure to praise your child for his efforts to become a stronger and more flexible thinker.

KEY POINTS TO REMEMBER

1. Before you teach your child the rational, self-control–enhancing coping statements in this chapter, talk to him or her about the concept of self-talk. Self-talk consists of the private thoughts we all have and use to guide and control our behavior.

2. Coach your child to use rational coping statements when he is calm or in the very early stages of emotional upset. If he or she really loses control of temper and behavior, a short time-out may be necessary. Once the tantrum has passed you can offer some rational coping statements for your

child to use the next time the same frustrating situation occurs.

3. Try to model flexible thinking and rational coping statements yourself.

4. Remember that it will take lots and lots of repetition, review, and practice for your child to learn flexible and rational thinking skills.

6
Self-Control Skills
Part II: Building Verbalization Skills

Many aggressive children are stunted in their ability to verbalize thoughts and feelings effectively or seem to have little faith in spoken language as a means of solving problems in relationships with friends, siblings, and parents. The more your child learns to verbalize feelings and to value language as a means of self-expression and as a tool for solving problems, the greater are the chances that his or her aggressive behaviors will decrease in frequency and intensity. This chapter discusses a range of techniques you can use to help your child develop better verbal and self-control skills. The methods described in this chapter will also help your child learn to value language as a way of sharing experiences, solving problems, and enhancing the quality of important relationships.

In using the following techniques please remember that the process of helping a defiant/aggressive child learn to use spoken language more effectively is just that—a process. It may take months or even years of effort on your part to help your child become verbally competent. The remainder of this chapter describes a number of methods to build verbalization skills in defiant children.

HAVING PLEASANT CONVERSATIONS
WITH YOUR CHILD

Pleasantly chatting with your child about day-to-day events, experiences, observations about people, and questions about the world is a good way to introduce him to the pleasures and multiple uses of spoken language. Creating fun, nonconflictual conversations with your child provides him the opportunity to share thoughts and feelings and to observe you sharing your thoughts and feelings about whatever topic is being discussed. You can initiate chats with your child in a variety of situations over the course of a normal day; for example, car rides, meal times, walks, housecleaning times, shopping trips. Conversations with your child may be only a few minutes in length or considerably longer if it suits the two of you.

The basics of this conversational technique are as follows. During the "chats" be sure not to dominate the discussion. It is important that your child sense that there is room for him to ask questions and offer opinions. If you talk too much your child may experience the talk as more of a lecture by you rather than a fun, shared experience. Every few minutes ask your child to elaborate on an idea or feeling he has expressed and wait to see if he can do so. Intermittently praise your child for sharing an idea or a feeling and let him know that you appreciate his good ideas and observations. Have a laugh over any silly or offbeat idea your child may put forward and try to speak to his or her personal creativity. Also, it is important that you be aware of your feelings while chatting with your child and that you freely share them. Your ability to model the healthy expression of thoughts and feelings gives your child a firsthand look at how to become verbally competent.

It is quite reasonable and even desirable for some of the discussions with your child to focus on the harder or more difficult aspects of life. For example, you might decide to talk about a frustrating or disappointing experience you had recently and how you were able to cope with it effectively. An elderly family member or pet might become seriously ill and die, thus stimulating conversation about illness and death. Your child might have a fight with a friend over the use of a bicycle, a situation that could lead to discussion about friendship and sharing. Your child might become aware of some frightening event in your community like a fire, a flood, or a tornado touching down. Unfortunate events such as these also provide many opportunities for you to encourage verbal competence in your child. Whether the conversations you have with your child are light and fun or on the more serious side, it is critical that you maintain an encouraging and respectful attitude toward his thoughts, feelings, opinions, complaints, and questions. Over time this shared conversational technique may help your child become a skilled conversationalist and more interested in using spoken language to solve problems. This technique will also greatly enhance the quality of your relationship with your child.

LEARNING TO SPEAK PREFERENTIALLY

Learning the art of preferential speech is one of the most important communication and interpersonal skills your child can learn. Helping children to speak preferentially literally means teaching them to use the words *prefer*, *like*, *wish*, and *want* when expressing thoughts and opinions. Many defiant and aggressive children don't have a clue as to how to speak preferentially and instead express opinions through angry, demanding attitudes that contain thoughts like "I *demand* to get my way," "I *must* never do hard things that make me feel uncomfortable," "I *demand* fair treatment all the time," "I *must* always have my fun," "There is only one way to do this—my way." To help defiant children give up verbally abusive behavior and demanding attitudes, I quickly encourage them to start saying things like "I'd strongly *prefer* to get my way now but I don't always have to get my way" or "I *wish* this homework wasn't so hard but it is—I can handle it," "I'd *prefer* fair treatment but unfair things often happen." Other examples of preferential speech are statements like, "Mom, I *want* [or would like] my sister to stop bothering me," or "Dad, I'd *prefer* to have pizza tonight," or "I'd *prefer* [or like] to ride my bike now." Preferential speech also means asking others about their preferences or desires. For example, Joey might say to a friend, "Brandon, would you *prefer* to play checkers or watch a video?"

To start this type of skill development with your child, first explain that you would like him to start using the words *prefer, want, like,* and *wish* more often and that you will use them as well. Tell your child that by learning to communicate thoughts and opinions as preferences rather than demands he will probably get his way more often since people generally respond more favorably to politely stated preferences than angry demands. Remind your child, however, that learning to speak preferentially does not guarantee that he will always get his way. It only means that his chances for getting his way are somewhat improved. As always, be sure to praise your child as he begins to utilize preferential, nondemanding attitudes and speech with you and with other people.

TEACHING YOUR CHILD ABOUT FEELINGS

In my clinical work with defiant children I almost always make it a point to evaluate how well they can identify and define several specific emotions, particularly sadness, worry, disappointment, frustration, embarrassment, envy, jealousy, anger, shame, and guilt. Not surprisingly, many of the children who come to see me need considerable help learning how to identify, define and express many or all of these feelings.

To help your child learn to identify and verbalize a fuller range of emotions, you first need to gain some sense of which emotions he already understands and can identify. After assessing your child's feelings vocabulary, offer clear, straightforward definitions and explanations of the specific new emotions your child needs to learn to notice and to verbalize. The definitions I typically use include a description of the feeling and the situations in which the feeling is likely to occur. To help you in your efforts to define specific feelings for your child, I now offer a quick review of the emotions mentioned above. Do your best to describe these particular feeling states in terms that are simple and straightforward so that your child is more likely to understand the definitions you offer.

SADNESS—Sadness is the lonely feeling of being down, blue, unhappy, or heartsick. Sad feelings often develop in children in relation to experiences of loss—death of a pet, death of a family member or friend, separation and divorce of parents, emotional or physical abandonment by a parent, loss of a friend's friendship.

WORRY—Worry is the nervous or fearful feeling that something bad is going to happen. When worried, many children experience either stomachache, headache, increased heart rate, sleep difficulty, sweating, shakiness, or some combination of these symptoms. Assuming there is no medical problem, I often tell children that these physical aches and pains are simply the body's way of telling the child that he is expecting some bad thing to happen. The feeling of worry arises when the child's sense of safety or emotional security is threatened by fears about physical safety; fears about receiving disapproval from parents, teachers, or friends; fears about parents being harmed in some way; fears about losing a parent; or fears about parents mistreating each other.

DISAPPOINTMENT—Disappointment is the sinking feeling of being let down in some way. Children experience the emotion of disappointment when trusted friends or family members break promises, when plans to have fun or to do something exciting are abandoned, or when a parent or other important person fails to follow through on some important commitment such as visiting or spending time with the child. Sadness frequently accompanies the emotion of disappointment because disappointing situations are also often tinged with a sense of loss.

FRUSTRATION—Frustration is the feeling of being uncomfortable or bothered, or the feeling that something is hard. The emotion of frustration is usually the immediate precursor to anger but it is not anger. Many defiant children see no difference between frustration and anger because these emotions usually tangle together very quickly. Nevertheless, it is important to try to help these children identify and verbalize the feeling of frustration as a separate emotion. Competent verbalization of frustration may prevent the emergence of full-blown anger or rage. Feelings of frustration occur when the child cannot get something he wants or is prevented from doing something he wants to do. Frustration is also experienced when a task is hard and requires sustained effort to complete. Teach your child to use the words *frustrated, bothered,* or *hard* to express frustration: "Mom, this homework is hard and it bothers me to do it. I feel frustrated."

EMBARRASSMENT—Embarrassment is the self-conscious feeling of a loss of confidence in oneself or of feeling silly, stupid, small, or inadequate in the eyes of others. Children experience embarrassment when they make mistakes in front of others, do not perform well on tasks or tests, say or do inappropriate things that bring on ridicule from others, or are teased or put down by peers or are put down in front of peers or parents.

ENVY—Envy is a two-person problem. That is, it is a problem that exists between your child and one other person. Envy is the resentful feeling that another person is in possession of some very desirable personal quality or thing that will never be accessible to the person feeling the envy. Envious feelings often give rise to feelings of contempt for the envied person and feelings of wanting to spoil the qualities, talents, or possessions of the envied person. Children may experience envy when they see others with more money, better houses, clothes, or toys, or when they see physical or personality characteristics or special talents in others they wish they had. Children also envy other children whom they see as having better family relationships or situations than their own may be.

JEALOUSY—Jealously is a three-person problem—that is, a problem that exists between your child and two other people. Jealously is a feeling that an important relationship is threatened by the presence of a rival. It is the resentful, suspicious feeling that a rival may influence a friend, parent, or other important person to pay more attention to the rival or have a more exclusive relationship with the rival than with the person feeling the jealousy. Children commonly feel jealous when siblings are born, when new children appear on the scene and start to horn in on existing peer relationships, when stepparents enter the picture, and even sometimes when parents want time alone together.

ANGER—Anger is a familiar feeling for most defiant children. In its more intense and unhealthy forms it is the feeling of wrath, fury, or rage arising in response to frustration or to some perceived injustice or sense of personal injury. In its milder, healthier forms it is the feeling of being annoyed, irritated, or resentful in relation to a situation of frustration, or a sense of being treated unfairly by others.

SHAME—Shame is the humiliating feeling of having lost the respect of others because of some inappropriate or improper behavior. It is the feeling of dishonor and disgrace over bad behavior that has been exposed for all to see.

GUILT—Although related to shame, guilt is a different emotion. It is the painful feeling of self-reproach or self-condemnation or remorse stemming from the belief that one has done something wrong or has acted in an immoral or unethical manner.

Look for opportunities to discuss the specific emotions your child needs to learn and to explain what each of these emotions means in terms that your child can understand. Furthermore, any time your child encounters a problem that might trigger one or several of these basic emotions, try to help him identify and verbalize the appropriate emotion that logically fits the triggering situation. Also, work very hard to notice and freely express each of these emotions as you experience them in day-to-day life. By learning how to identify and verbalize these basic emotions, your child will be better able to express painful states of mind with less anger. I elaborate on this point in the next section.

ANGER: THE ALL-PURPOSE EMOTION OF DEFIANT CHILDREN

Anger is the "all-purpose" or "one size fits all" emotion of defiant children. Almost any type of hassle, frustration, or relationship problem seems to elicit from these children an angry tirade of verbal abuse and often some type of aggressive acting out that is designed to control or eliminate the situation of frustration, whatever it may be.

I have many times asked the children I treat whether they have ever felt angry and at the same time felt that nobody understood their point of view or their side of the story. Invariably the answer is yes. I explain to my young patients that the reason that parents, teachers, friends, and siblings don't understand them is that they always start to deal with hassles by skipping over first feelings and expressing only second feelings of anger and resentment. I then show them a chart of first and second feelings (see Table 6–1) and explain that in virtually all difficult situation they first have feelings of sadness, worry, jealousy, embarrassment, frustration, shame, disappointment, envy, or guilt, and then second feelings of anger and resentment. I also mention that sometimes people simply have first feelings without anger. Next I explain the link between first and second feelings by pointing out that children often get angry at the people who make them feel sad, frustrated, worried, embarrassed, jealous, dis-

TABLE 6–1. First and Second Feelings

First Feelings	Second Feelings
Sadness	
Worry	
Disappointment	*Unhealthy Anger*—Rage, fury,
Frustration	wrath
Embarrassment	
Envy	*Healthy Anger*—Annoyance,
Jealousy	resentment, milder anger
Shame	
Guilt	

Be aware that guilt, shame, sadness, or embarrassment may also be experienced by your child after an inappropriate display of anger.

appointed, envious, and so on. I then suggest to the child that if he would try to express first and second feelings in the correct order, he might actually feel that others better understand the depth of his upset. Thus he might not have to get so angry to try to get others to respond to the first feelings that he often keeps hidden behind his rage. This explanation usually makes sense to the children I counsel. Finally I offer concrete examples of how to express first and second feelings based on recent episodes of temper or upset from the child's life. For example, "Kyle, I think you felt disappointed when your mother said you couldn't rent a video and you felt mad at her too," or "Mary, I bet you were embarrassed when Theresa teased you and you were also angry at her."

You can teach your child about first and second feelings using the same chart and explanation I use. As always, try to model the healthy expression of first and second feelings as you experience them in your day-to-day situations of frustration. For example, you might share stories about situations in which you first felt disappointed and then angry or in which you first felt embarrassed and then resentful. Modeling this skill is important to your child's overall emotional and psychological growth. After you have introduced your child to the chart of first and second feelings and explained how they connect to each other, it may take time for your child to catch on and use this skill. In fact, your child may not catch on at all and may instead continue to use anger as the all-purpose emotion for every situation of frustration. If your child's anger continues unabated, you can still try to help him learn to verbalize first and second feelings more competently by waiting for temper tantrums to pass and then conducting an after-the-fact review of first and second feelings. Here are some examples of how to coach your child to identify and verbalize first and second feelings both before and after the fact.

Examples

Dad and Jason are on their way to a soccer game and Jason is hoping his team will win this important playoff match. Dad says, "Jason, I hope your team wins today, but if not, I want you to try to tell me your first and second feelings about not winning. Many boys would feel bothered, disappointed, and angry about losing an important game. But remember, I do hope you win the game."

Mary is screaming, yelling, and slamming doors because her mother will not let her watch TV until her homework is done. After the tantrum is over and Mary has regained self-control, her mother offers the following comments. "Mary, I think you were feeling very bothered and frustrated about not getting TV time and you were also angry at me. I hope that the next time that you are frustrated and angry you will try harder to put your feelings into words. Then we can try to talk the problem out."

Dad calls to tell George that he has to work late and will not be able to take George out for pizza as planned. Several minutes after the call George throws a glass against the kitchen wall where it smashes into many pieces. After he calms down, Mom says, "George, I think you were feeling very disappointed that Dad had to cancel his dinner plan with you and you were also very angry at him for disappointing you in this way. The next time someone disappoints you I hope you can put your upset into words. That way you can still be upset but stay out of trouble."

VERBALIZING THE WISH TO ACT OUT

Many defiant and aggressive children do not realize that spoken language gives them the ability to verbalize the wish to act out aggressively without having to do so. I have often encouraged the children I see to verbalize the wish to act out as long as they also add a self-control statement to the verbalized aggressive wish. For example, a child who has been breaking property might be encouraged to say something like, "I'm so mad I feel like I want to kick a hole in the wall but I'm not going to." A child who repeatedly hits her younger sister might be encouraged to say, "My sister bothers me so much I feel like I want to hit her but I won't." A verbally abusive child might learn to say, "I'm so mad at you I feel like I want to swear and call you names but I'm going to control myself." By learning how to verbalize the wish to act out, aggressive children discover a new way to express the depth of their anger without getting into trouble.

USE A DAILY FEELINGS DIARY

The technique of using a daily feelings diary with your child has previously been discussed by Bloomquist (1996). The method I use is quite easy and straightforward to use. Purchase a small notepad for your child and explain that you would like to see if once a day he could write down a tough situation, for example, "I was teased by some kids at school," and then note first and second feelings, such as "I was embarrassed and then I felt mad." You might even put an outline on the pages of the notepad so that your child is clear about what you want him to do. At the top of each page write "Tough Situation" with some lines beneath for your child to write his description of the problem. In the middle of the page write "First Feelings" and at the bottom of the page write "Second Feelings." Then you're all set to get started (see Table 6–2). If your child resists the idea of the daily feelings diary, do not force the issue. Instead, use only the other verbal skill-building methods described in this chapter. If your child is willing to try to keep a feelings diary, set up a regular time to meet each day to review your child's entry and

TABLE 6–2. My Feelings Diary

Name:_____   Date:_____

1. Tough Situation: _____
_____
_____
_____

2. My First Feelings: _____
_____
_____
_____

3. My Second Feelings: _____
_____
_____
_____

offer encouragement, support, and praise for any steps
he makes toward identifying his feelings and thoughts
about difficult situations.

LEARNING TO TALK IT OUT

The methods described in this chapter will help your child
learn to "talk it out" rather than "act it out" or "shout it
out." Each day as problems arise encourage your child
to talk it out and to freely express thoughts, preferences,
opinions, first and second feelings, and his ideas about
how to solve problems in constructive ways. Be sure to
praise and reinforce any and all efforts your child makes

to use language as a tool for resolving conflicts with others and for coping with the frustrations of daily life.

KEY POINTS TO REMEMBER

1. You can influence your child to gain skill at verbalizing thoughts and feelings if you have regular, nonconflictual conversations with him; model the healthy expression of first and second feelings; teach the connection between first and second feelings; help your child understand the meaning of different emotions; encourage verbalization of the wish to act out; and encourage the use of a daily feelings diary. Over time these multiple methods of influence may improve your child's ability to rely on spoken language as the primary means for solving problems and expressing himself.

2. Be sure to praise your child's efforts to express ideas and feelings.

3. Do not criticize offbeat ideas expressed by your child. Try to put a positive spin on such ideas as being "creative," or respond with good-natured humor.

7

Self-Control Skills

Part III: Building Impulse-Control, Problem-Solving, and Tease-Tolerance Skills

The hassles in the lives of aggressive children occur largely as a result of their impulsive nature and limited repertoire of problem-solving skills. When frustrated, these children quickly resort to defiance, yelling, hitting, breaking things, swearing, and pushing and never seem to learn from experience how to better control themselves or solve problems more effectively. In this chapter you will learn techniques to help your child develop better impulse control when frustrated or provoked and a problem-solving formula you can teach your child to use to solve problems more effectively. Toward the end of this chapter I also discuss a specific tease-tolerance method I have developed to help children maintain self-control when teased by siblings and peers and I offer some thoughts on how to help your child make good choices regarding behavior, attitudes, and problem-solving efforts.

DEVELOPING IMPULSE-CONTROL AND PROBLEM-SOLVING SKILLS

To get your child started on the road to better impulse control, it is important to again introduce him to the idea of self-talk or self-guiding statements. Self-guiding statements are the private thoughts that all humans use to direct thinking, behavior, and problem-solving efforts, and to evaluate personal performance at any given moment. To help your child grasp this concept, offer a clear, straight-forward definition of self-talk and give examples of your own self-talk in a variety of situations. Below is a conversation between Ellen and her 9-year-old son Jake, who has displayed aggressive behavior for years. Ellen is introducing Jake to the concept of self-talk.

> "Jake, before we talk about ways for you to have more self-control and to make better problem-solving choices, I want to talk to you about something called self-talk. Self-talk is something that all kids and grownups do all the time but nobody sees. Self-talk means the private thoughts that you have in your mind about your behavior and about what is going on around you. For example, when you feel hungry you probably think something like, 'It's time to get a snack.' That thought is your self-talk. I have self-talk too. This morning when I woke up I began to think about what I had to do today, so I thought to myself, 'I have to do the laundry and pay the bills. I'd better get up and get going or my work won't get done.' That was my self-talk. Kids and parents also have self-talk in tough situations. For example, when our neighbor Mr. Williams came over yesterday and yelled at me because the leaves from our yard blew into his yard, I was thinking 'This guy is really annoying. I'd like to tell him off right now but I won't.' That was

my self-talk and I used it to help me have self-control even when I was feeling angry at Mr. Williams. Kids can learn all kinds of self-talk to help improve self-control in tough situations and to help them choose better ways of solving problems. That's what I want to teach you now: new types of self-talk that you can use to help yourself stay out of trouble and to get along better with other kids and with Dad and me."

After your child understands the basic idea of self-talk, you can then teach him the following impulse-control and problem-solving method described by a number of investigators (Kendall and Braswell 1993, Nelson and Finch 1996). Your child can use the following method to deal with all kinds of frustrating situations and social problems. Also, remember to offer frequent stop and think prompts and reminders whenever your child is heading into a potentially explosive situation.

Step 1. *Stop and think!*—The goal of this step is to help your child interrupt his seemingly automatic aggressive responses long enough to consider alternate ways of solving problems. To help your child learn this critically important first step, encourage him to imagine several specific frustrating situations that typically elicit his aggressive responses and tell him that these are exactly the times to incorporate the words "stop and think" into his self-talk.

Step 2. *What is the problem?*—This step is designed to give your child a chance to identify and define the problem in clear and simple terms.

Step 3. *What are some possible solutions?*—At this stage your child generates three possible solutions to his problem. He is encouraged not to select a solution until he carefully considers each of the three solutions he has generated.

Step 4. *What are the possible consequences or outcomes of each solution?*—Your child is now encouraged to anticipate the likely impact and outcome of each of the solutions he has generated.

Step 5. *Pick the best solution and use it.*—At this stage your child makes a choice based on his sense of which solution stands the best chance of solving his problem with the least risk of getting into trouble.

Step 6. *How did the solution work?*—The final step in this impulse-control and problem-solving procedure involves having the child step back and make a judgment about how well the solution worked. If it worked well, your child is encouraged to praise himself for a job well done. If the plan did not work, he is encouraged to go back to Step 1 and use the same process all over again to find yet another possible solution to the current problem.

Here is an example of how Jake eventually learned to use this procedure after much trial and error, practice and repetition.

Ellen is taking Jake to a Halloween party knowing that several of the boys at the party are aggressive and at times cruel to other children. On the way Ellen helps Jake anticipate that there might be trouble with some of these kids. She then reviews the impulse-control and problem-solving procedure with Jake and asks him to restate the procedure to himself in case he needs to use it at the party.

At the party two of the boys decide to play a practical joke on Jake. As one boy talks to Jake, the other boy sneaks up behind him and stuffs ice cubes down his shirt. Both of these jokesters then burst out laughing at Jake's visible discomfort. Although Jake is furious, he remembers his impulse control and problem-solving plan. A slow motion picture of Jake's self-talk at this difficult moment looks like this.

1. "Stop and think!"

2. "What's the problem? The problem is these guys are being mean to me."

3. "What are some solutions? I could beat them up; I could be a good sport about the joke and act like I don't care all that much; I could get help from one of the adults."

4. "What are the consequences of each of these three solutions? If I try to beat them up I'll get into

trouble and I'll miss out on the rest of the party. If I
stuff my feelings and act like I don't care I'll stay out
of trouble and the other kids might think I'm pretty
cool. If I go tell the adults the kids at the party might
think I'm a tattletale."

5. "Which solution do I want to use? I'll pretend
to go along with the joke, be a good sport, and act
like I don't really care about the ice down my shirt."
Jake selects this solution and uses it.

6. A few minutes later Jake asks himself, "How
did it work? This worked! I didn't get into trouble
and I'm still having fun at the party. One of the adults
noticed what those boys did to me and they got
scolded. That's good enough for me. I did a good
job handling this problem." Jake's mother agreed
since she had witnessed the incident. A few minutes later Ellen pulled Jake aside and praised him
for self-control and competent problem-solving
efforts.

DEVELOPING TEASE-TOLERANCE

Your child can use the problem-solving method just described to cope more effectively with teasing by siblings
or peers. Alternatively, you can teach your child the following four-step method I have developed to help children keep their cool when provoked or teased by other
children or their siblings. A number of the children I see

tell me that this tease-tolerance technique works quite well (see Table 7–1).

Before I discuss the actual technique I would like to mention that many parents often advise their children to "just ignore" kids who tease and taunt them. Most of the time this advice does not work because the children are too agitated and angry to be able to "just ignore" teasing by others. To be able to ignore effectively your child has to have some powerful imagery that illustrates how his angry overreactions play right into the hands of the child doing the teasing and he has to learn several mental steps to use before he ignores the teasing.

To teach your child my tease-tolerance technique, first ask him to picture a marionette puppet on strings. Tell your child that when he angrily overreacts to teasing by others it is just as if he had tied strings to his arms, legs, and voice box and handed them to the child who is doing the teasing. The child doing the teasing then feels very powerful, keeps pulling the strings, and greatly enjoys the angry show put on by your child. When you describe

TABLE 7–1. The 4 Steps to Tease-Tolerance

1. *"Cool" thoughts to lower anger and strengthen self-control*
   "I can handle this."   "I'm a good person."
2. *Self-control booster thought*
   "I'm not his or her puppet—no show today!"
3. *Be assertive once and once only*
   "Stop teasing me. I don't like it."
4. *Ignore, resume play, or go for help from an adult*

this scene to your child be sure to emphasize what great entertainment his screaming and gesturing is for the child who is being mean or cruel. Let this image sink in for a moment and then ask your child if he wants other children to have this kind of power over him. It is very likely that your child will immediately say no. Next, ask him if he wants to learn how to take power away from the children who tease him. With this image in mind he will quickly say yes. Now the stage is set to teach him the four steps to tease-tolerance.

Step 1. *Think some "cool" thoughts for self-control*— "I can handle this," "I can keep my cool," "I'm still a good person."

Step 2. *Take power away from that kid by thinking the following power-busters thought*—"I'm not his puppet, no show today!"

Step 3. *Be assertive and stand up for yourself*—One time and one time only tell the boy or girl who is doing the teasing to stop the teasing or name calling because you don't like it. Be sure to remind your child to be polite when he stands up for himself. If the other child mocks him or imitates him at this step, tell him to again think the power-busters thought, "I'm not his puppet, no show today."

Step 4. *Walk away from the child who is doing the teasing and ignore any further rude or cruel remarks*—

Finally, tell your child that once he gets to Stage 4 and walks away, the other child may tease him even more to try to get the entertainment he wants. If your child resists the urge to react to the intensified teasing, he now has all the power and he gets the last laugh.

HELPING YOUR CHILD MAKE GOOD CHOICES REGARDING ATTITUDES AND BEHAVIOR

At this point you can begin to talk to your child about good versus bad choices regarding attitudes and behavior. Point out that bad choices—yelling, hitting, swearing—always lead to bad results. Explain to your child that when he chooses to lose control and lash out at others he pays a huge price. For such behavior the bad results always include getting into trouble, making the problem worse, getting a reputation as a difficult person or a hothead, feeling bad or guilty afterwards, and doing damage to important relationships. Emphasize that a choice to lose control and to act impulsively and aggressively is always also a choice to bring on all of the above-mentioned bad results. That's the rule (see Table 7–2).

Now talk to your child about good choices and good results. Explain that a choice to stay in control and to use the thinking, impulse-control, and problem-solving skills that have been taught almost always leads to good results. The good results include staying out of trouble, improving the chances of getting your own way (though there

TABLE 7–2. Good vs. Bad Choices

	Bad Choice	*=*	*Bad Results*
Negative Solutions	Yelling		Makes problem worse
	Hitting		Get into trouble
	Not thinking		Feel guilty or bad
	Breaking things		Reputation as hothead
	Slamming		Damage relation-
	Screaming		ships
	Good Choice	*=*	*Good Results*
Positive Solutions	Self-control		Sometimes get your way
	Express anger politely		Feel proud of self
	Flexible thinking		Stay out of trouble
	Use words and ideas		Reputation of being mature
	Compromise		Preserve relation- ships

is never any guarantee that your child will get his own way even if he does make a good choice), feeling proud of staying in control, getting a reputation of being grown-up and mature, and strengthening important relationships. Emphasize that a choice to stay in control and to use words and ideas to solve problems is always also a choice to get some good results. That's the rule (see Table 7–2).

If you have worked to teach your child all of the self-control methods discussed in this chapter and in Chapters 5 and 6, you are now free to define all subsequent behavior displayed by your child as a matter of personal choice. This does not mean that you stop reviewing, practicing, and prompting the use of new thinking and problem-solving skills, or that you now blame your child for bad choices regarding behavior and attitudes. It only means that you consistently and compassionately let your child know that he or she has a choice to make in any difficult situation and that you hope he or she can find the strength to make good choices. If your child continues to choose oppositional, defiant, and aggressive behaviors and attitudes, however, it is critical that you not give up on your relationship with him or her. Remember, your child is always and unconditionally a worthwhile person, even when he or she continues to make bad choices.

The material in this chapter is designed to help you help your child learn impulse control, problem-solving, and tease-tolerance skills. In working with your child on these areas of skill development please remember that a great deal of repetition, review, prompting, and reinforcement is necessary for your child to learn, internalize, and use these adaptive, prosocial problem-solving methods.

KEY POINTS TO REMEMBER

1. To strengthen your child's impulse-control and problem-solving skills, teach him or her to stop and

think, define the problem, generate three solutions, anticipate the likely outcome of each solution, pick the best solution and use it, and evaluate how the solution worked.

2. As your child begins to show better impulse control and problem-solving skills, encourage him or her to administer self-praise for handling tough situations.

3. A great deal of repetition of the impulse-control and problem-solving formula is necessary for your child to use this method effectively.

8
Monitoring Progress

An ongoing plan to monitor your child's progress will help him maintain his behavioral improvement. To monitor progress effectively you need to set clear goals for your child, establish a daily meeting in which progress toward goals is discussed, and encourage your child to report more accurately on his or her behavior. The first section of this chapter will help you select your child's daily goals and map the specific strategies you will use to help him or her achieve these goals. The final section gives you tools to help your child self-monitor his behavior and to accurately reflect or report on it.

IDENTIFYING BEHAVIORAL GOALS

To identify social and behavioral goals for your child, you first need to review his or her main behavioral problems or "symptoms," such as physical aggression, lying, and oppositional behavior. Inappropriate problem behaviors like these can be viewed as indicators of specific skill weaknesses in your child (Strayhorn 1988). For example, a child who is cruel and aggressive toward others is relatively weak in the skill of being kind and gentle to others. Lying reflects relative weakness in the skill of giving accurate and truthful answers. An oppositional/defiant attitude reflects some weakness in the skill of following directions and maintaining a cooperative/respectful attitude, and so forth.

As your child becomes more competent in the specific skill areas that you will identify as his high-priority "skill goals," his main behavioral problems should fade significantly. Table 8–1 lists some of the problem behaviors that oppositional children typically display. Next to each problem behavior is the desired social or behavioral skill required to reduce the symptomatic behavior. Select three or four of the skills you most want your child to display right away and use them as the first set of high-priority skill-goals for your child to work on. As your child begins to display competence in one or several of the initial skill areas, you can add new goals to the workplan. If your child has a particular problem that is not identified in Table 8–1, a consultation with a behaviorally oriented therapist might help you develop other specific prosocial goals.

THE HIGH-PRIORITY SKILLS WORKPLAN

After selecting your child's goals, you can write a high-priority skills workplan using a form like the one displayed in Table 8–2. This format allows you to record your child's main symptoms, list his or her high-priority skill goals, identify the specific methods of influence you will use to help him or her achieve these goals, and remain focused

TABLE 8–1. Symptoms/Skills Menu

Symptoms	Skill-Goals
1. Not following directions	1. Following directions
2. Defiant talk/verbal abuse	2. Respectful talk
3. Cruelty and aggression toward others	3. Kind and gentle with others
4. Lying	4. Accurate and truthful answers
5. Stealing/property destruction	5. Respect for others' property
6. "Poor sport" when frustrated (low frustration tolerance), includes tantruming, arguing, badgering	6. "Good sport" when frustrated (high frustration tolerance), good-natured acceptance of not getting own way
7. Acting before thinking (impulsivity)	7. Thinking before acting (impulse control)
8. Swearing	8. Clean talk
9. Cheating	9. Playing fair
10. Not sharing	10. Sharing with others
11. Blaming others	11. Admitting mistakes
12. Not talking about ideas and feelings	12. Talking about ideas and feelings
13. Teasing peers	13. Talking nicely to peers
14. Screaming/making loud voices	14. Talking in a normal tone of voice
15. Rigid thinking	15. Flexible thinking
16. Interrupting	16. Listening to others
17. Bossiness with others	17. Letting others have their way
18. Demanding attitudes	18. Preferential attitudes
19. Insulting others	19. Complimenting others
20. Ignoring people	20. Paying attention to others
21. Oppositional attitude	21. Cooperative attitude

TABLE 8–2. High-Priority Skills Work Plan

| Child's Name | Kyle | | Age | 8 | | Date of this Plan | 7/7/99 |

Problem Areas
1) Physical aggression toward others   2) Poor sport when frustrated
3) Noncompliant and oppositional re: chores & tasks   4) Defiant talk

			PARENTAL METHODS OF INFLUENCE		
Skills (Goals for Child)		Consequences	Modeling	Practice & Review	Other Methods of Influence
1. Kind & gentle with others	→	Enthusiastic attention	Parents model kindness and concern for others	1) All family interaction 2) Daily review of goals	1) Nightly review 2) Proudly discuss child's progress 3) No violent TV or cartoons 4) Stories & videos with kindness themes
(Physical aggression→)		Automatic time-out			
2. Good sport when frustrated	→	Enthusiastic attention	Parents model being good sports when frustrated	1) All family interaction 2) Daily review of goals	1) Nightly review 2) Proudly discuss child's progress 3) Review self-control thoughts
(Poor sport	→)	Ignore			

3. Follow directions / Cooperative attitude	→ Enthusiastic attention	Parents model cooperative attitudes	1) All family interaction 2) Daily review of goals	1) Nightly review 2) Proudly discuss child's progress 3) Compliance training 4) 20 min. special time each day
(Noncompliant	→) Command-warning Time-out			
4. Respectful talk	→ Enthusiastic attention	Parents model respectful talk	1) All family interaction 2) Daily review of goals	1) Nightly review 2) Proudly discuss child's progress 3) Review self-control thoughts
(Defiant talk	→) Ignore			

Adapted from *The Competent Child: An Approach to Psychotherapy and Preventive Mental Health* by J. M. Strayhorn, copyright © 1988 by Guilford Publications. Used by permission of the publisher.

on all aspects of the plan. The instructions for completing the workplan are as follows.

1. *The problem area lines*—On these lines note the three or four main symptoms you see as major problem areas for your child. Remember, these symptoms reflect specific skill weaknesses in your child.

2. *The skill-goals column*—In the skill-goals column list the three or four high-priority skills you want your child to learn. In the parentheses under each high-priority skill list the related symptom again.

3. *The consequences column*—In this column list the positive consequences you will provide your child when he or she displays the desired high-priority skill (e.g., praise or enthusiastic attention). At the bottom of the box, next to the line in parentheses, list the negative consequences you will use when the unwanted symptom or problem emerges (e.g., ignoring or time-out).

4. *The practice and review column*—In the practice and review column list "all family interaction" as a reminder to yourself that in all family interaction you have numerous opportunities to work on, practice, and model the high-priority skills you want your child to learn. In this column you can also note that you will conduct a daily review of your child's goals and progress.

5. *The other methods of influence column*—In this column list several other positive methods of influence that may help your child learn his high-priority skills more rapidly. For example, you could list the nightly review technique, the technique of proudly discussing your child's progress with his other parent, the technique of removing aggressive or violent television, and compliance training. Sometimes parents add additional techniques such as reading or viewing children's stories and videos that contain kindness themes or themes of cooperation, sharing, telling the truth, and so forth (Strayhorn 1988).

Guidelines for Using the High-Priority Skills Workplan

1. Once you have selected your child's goals, review with him the specific skills you want him to practice each day. Establishing clear goals for your child will help him know the specific behaviors and attitudes you want him to display more frequently. At the end of this discussion post your child's goals in his room using a form like the one in Table 8–3.

2. Post the entire skills workplan where you are likely to see it every day as a cue to keep yourself focused on all of the plan's components. Once a week review the entire plan to keep yourself firmly on track.

TABLE 8–3. Child Self-Report

How did I do today?   Today's Date _____

My goals are:

1. Kind and gentle with others

2. Good sport when frustrated

3. Follow directions/cooperative attitude

4. Respectful talk

Today on Goal 1 I did → very well — OK — not so hot

Today on Goal 2 I did → very well — OK — not so hot

Today on Goal 3 I did → very well — OK — not so hot

Today on Goal 4 I did → very well — OK — not so hot

    1. If you did pretty well on your goals today, pat yourself on the back and tell yourself: "I did a good job today!"

    2. If you had a hard day today, talk to your parents about how you can stay out of trouble and make tomorrow a better day.

    3. Remember, even if you had problems today, you are always a good person.

    3. At least once a week provide feedback to your child's other parent on how well he or she is following the plan and ask him or her to give you feedback on how you are doing. Don't get defensive if you receive criticism. Use the criticism to correct your behavior so that you can forcefully and consistently implement the methods of influence listed on the workplan.

ENCOURAGING ACCURATE SELF-REFLECTION

Children who display oppositional, defiant, and aggressive behavior frequently blame others for their problems and deny or minimize their own behavioral difficulties. This tendency to externalize responsibility for problems is generally a source of great frustration for parents because the child acts as if he has no responsibility for his inappropriate actions. Out of frustration, parents sometimes resort to lectures, interrogation, yelling, and a variety of other coercive methods to browbeat the child into admitting mistakes and taking responsibility for his bad behavior. Such methods generally backfire and instead push the child to blame others even more, especially the angry, accusing parents.

To help a defiant child learn to take responsibility for his or her actions and develop the capacity for self-reflection, a gentler method is needed. A less confrontational approach will reduce the chances of your child's becoming angry and defensive and will create a more positive atmosphere within which all behavior can be examined and understood. The method I recommend to promote self-reflection in defiant children is a modified version of a psychotherapy technique designed to help impulsive children develop the skill of accurate self-evaluation (Kendall and Braswell 1993). The goal of this technique is to reinforce the accuracy of your child's self-report on his or her behavior.

To monitor your child's progress on his daily goals and help him develop the capacity for accurate self-reflection, use the following method.

1. Take a few minutes at the end of each day to compare notes with your child on how well he practiced his high-priority skills that day. Before you meet with your child complete a parent report form like the one displayed in Table 8–4. As you rate your child's progress on each of his goals, be sure to note the specific behavioral evidence you are using as the basis of your rating.

2. During your meeting with your child, calmly and supportively ask him to review his goals and then, using a child self-report form like the one displayed in Table 8–3, ask him to circle and discuss the rating that best describes his behavior that day in relation to each specific goal. (If your child cannot yet read, omit the forms and follow these guidelines using a discussion format only.) For example, as Chris circles "very well" on practicing kindness, he tells his mother that he thinks he did quite well showing kindness toward his sister.

3. Next, share your report with your child. Remember, provide feedback in a supportive manner. Chris's mother replies: "Chris, I agree with your report. I think you did very well practicing kindness today because I

TABLE 8-4. Parent Report

How did my child do today?   Today's Date _____

1. Kind and gentle with others _____

2. Good sport when frustrated _____

3. Follow directions/cooperative attitude _____

4. Respectful talk _____

Today on Goal 1 he/she did → very well — OK — not so hot
(Evidence? _____)

Today on Goal 2 he/she did → very well — OK — not so hot
(Evidence? _____)

Today on Goal 3 he/she did → very well — OK — not so hot
(Evidence? _____)

Today on Goal 4 he/she did → very well — OK — not so hot
(Evidence? _____)

1. If any portion of your child's self-report matches any of
your ratings of his goals (whether he did well or poorly), praise
him for giving an accurate report on that goal or goals.

2. If your child gives an inaccurate self-report (e.g., he claims
good behavior on a day when many problems occurred), gently
encourage him to think again about what happened. If your child
does not come up with an accurate report, provide him with your
feedback. Then tell your child that tomorrow you and he will have
another chance to compare notes on his behavior.

3. For any problem area rated "OK" or "not so hot," discuss
with your child an adaptive problem-solving plan that he can use
tomorrow should the same difficult situation occur.

4. Remember, do not criticize, blame, or lecture your child
during the self-reflection discussion.

saw you help your sister when she fell down and scraped her knee." If Chris had instead circled "not so hot" for kindness his mother might say something like: "Chris, I agree. Today it looked to me like you were not very kind to your sister because when she fell down and scraped her knee you laughed at her. Good job reporting on your behavior."

4. If any portion of your child's self-report matches any of your ratings of his goals, praise him for giving an accurate report on that goal or goals. For example, if your child acknowledges that he was not kind to others today, praise him for truthfully reporting on his behavior: "Chris, you did a good job telling me that you were not kind to your sister today. I'm very proud of you for giving a truthful report."

5. If your child gives an inaccurate self-report (e.g., he claims good behavior on a day when many problems occurred), gently encourage him to think again about his behavior. If he does not produce an accurate report, provide him with your feedback. Then tell your child that tomorrow will bring another chance to compare notes on his behavior: "Okay, Chris, I guess you and I see things differently today. I think you were not kind to your sister because you kept calling her nasty names. I hope that tomorrow you will try harder to be kind to her. Tomorrow after dinner we'll review your goals again."

6. Remember, do not criticize, blame, scold, or lecture your child during the self-reflection discussion.

7. For any problem area that you and your child both rate as "OK" or "not so hot," discuss an adaptive problem-solving plan that he can use tomorrow should the same difficult situation occur again.

Over time this supportive technique may help your child begin to reflect and accurately report on his behavior, both good and bad. It will probably take much repetition of this particular method to show results. Do not be discouraged if your child does not give accurate self-reports right away.

A FEW FINAL TIPS

To sustain your child's behavioral recovery keep the following points in mind.

1. For some oppositional, defiant, and aggressive children the path toward recovery is characterized by alternating phases of improvement and brief flare-ups of disruptive behavior. In other words, progress usually occurs in a "two steps forward, one step backward" format. Do not be discouraged when this happens. Just keep using the techniques you have learned in this book. Over time, the flare-ups of disruptive behavior displayed by your child should occur less frequently.

2. As time goes by some parents start to forget about their child management plan or drift away from the use of positive social reinforcement for good behavior and penalties for bad behavior. At least once a month ask yourself: "Am I consistently using all of the methods of influence I have learned to help my child learn new behaviors and attitudes?" If your answer is no, reread this book. If your answer is yes, take yourself and a friend out to dinner.

3. Keep your child management plan in place when you are on vacation and during the summertime.

4. Remember, keep your anger under control, be playful with your child, remain optimistic about his or her future, and find ways to get out of the house and have some fun for yourself. There really is more to life than just raising children.

5. Parents are in control of many methods of influence to help an oppositional/defiant child learn new behaviors, attitudes, and ways of thinking about day-to-day problems. If you use the method described in this book consistently for twelve weeks, you will probably see substantial improvement in your child's behavior. If not, consult a child mental health professional for additional help, and do not lose hope. Finally, as you work with your child each day keep the following idea in mind:

"A diamond is just a piece of coal that stuck to its job." I hope all goes well for your and your child.

KEY POINTS TO REMEMBER

1. Set clear social, behavioral, and attitudinal goals for your child and review them with your child on a daily basis.
2. In your own day-to-day performance be sure to model or display the same social and behavioral skills you want your child to learn.
3. On your high-priority skills workplan map all of the methods of influence you will use to help your child achieve his or her goals and stick to the plan for at least three months. If you get good results from the specific child management techniques you have chosen to use, keep using them far into the future.
4. To help your child report more accurately on behavior meet with him or her each day to review progress toward goals and to praise the accuracy of his or her self-reports.
5. Look for every opportunity to create a warm, loving relationship with your child.

APPENDIX
Guidelines
for Clinicians

Although this book may be used by parents as a self-help resource, it was also designed to be a parent training manual for clinicians. Therapists specializing in the treatment of children, particularly children with disruptive behavior disorders, will find the approach I have developed to be a helpful first stage of intervention for many oppositional, defiant, and aggressive children. Because the text of this manual can be easily read by parents, it also supports a focused collaboration between parents and therapists toward a common goal—the rapid behavioral recovery of a defiant/aggressive child.

Before I discuss aspects of technique related to each of the eight chapters or stages of this intervention, I will offer a few general comments and guidelines for clinicians.

1. This parent training intervention is indicated for any 2- to 11-year-old child diagnosed with an externalizing or disruptive behavior disorder. It is contraindicated in cases in which a child's parent has a mental illness, substance abuse problem, or marital problem so severe that it would prevent the parent from learning and applying the skills described. In such situations these problems should be treated first.

2. The book supports a skills-based treatment for parents. It was written specifically to help parents acquire and maintain new methods of influence to promote social, behavioral, and attitudinal competence in their children.

3. To help parents learn new skills faster and use them longer, that is, further into the future, the concurrent use of readings, discussion, homework, in-session role play, and videos is recommended.

4. When parents are being trained in child management methods, it is helpful for the therapist to define his or her role as a teacher, consultant, philosopher, and coach.

5. It is generally advisable for clinicians to remain focused initially on behavioral improvement and stabilization for the child. Behavioral improvement usually helps children feel substantially better, and it goes a long

way toward improving the quality of the parent–child relationship.

6. Once the child has started to display improved behavior, clinicians, in consultation with parents, can decide whether additional treatment is needed to address other family or intrapsychic issues that may be affecting the child adversely.

7. The method detailed in this book can be used in conjunction with any type of individual psychotherapy that is being provided to the child, for example, cognitive-behavioral psychotherapy, psychodynamic psychotherapy, or psychoanalysis.

8. This parent training intervention can be conducted with parents individually or in a parent training group format.

9. The effectiveness of this intervention will be influenced by a number of variables, including the degree to which parents are able to learn new child management skills, the nature and severity of the child's disorder, and the nature and severity of disturbance in a parent.

My initial start-to-finish involvement with a child who has a disruptive behavior disorder typically lasts eight to fifteen weeks and is divided into five distinct phases, described below. Phases two through four can be lengthened or shortened as dictated by the parents' progress in mastering new child management skills and by the response of the child to the parent training intervention. The phases are *Diagnostic Evaluation* (one to two sessions), *Getting Ready for Change* (one to three sessions), *Parent Training in Child Management Methods* (three to five sessions), *Introducing the Child to Self-Control Skills* (three to five sessions), and *Aftercare Phase* (booster sessions as needed). These five phases capture the basic structure of my approach.

Questions sometimes arise about what to tell a child about a parent training intervention. After I have evaluated a child and determined that he or she might benefit from the method described in this book, I meet with the parents to share the results of my evaluation and my recommendation for a parent training intervention. If the parents agree to this recommendation, I tell the child that I enjoyed meeting him, that I can see that he is a boy (or girl) who very much wants to do well, and that his parents and I will try to help him do better. I also tell the child that I will not be seeing him for a month or two, but that I will be meeting with his parents to think about ways to help him solve his problems. I have found that most children are quite accepting of this arrangement, and when they return to sessions some six to eight weeks later they generally have no problem relating to me or engaging in the treatment.

I will now offer a few points on technique related to the eight chapters of this book. Typically I ask parents to read the chapter associated with the training before attending the relevant training session. Sessions begin with a review of the parents' comprehension of the concepts and techniques to be covered that week. Based on this assessment I make immediate judgments about how to shape the training session to best meet each parent's individual learning needs or to deal with irrational beliefs and emotional blocks related to the use of specific child management strategies.

Chapter 1—*Getting Ready for Change*: After parents read this first section I use Table 1–1, the "Parent 'Preflight' Checklist," to structure the session. As parents review this list of topics, I ask which areas, if any, they believe they need to work on to improve the chances that the child management techniques they will learn in later chapters will be effective. This usually leads to a straightforward discussion of individual factors that will help or hinder efforts to change and to promote improved behavior in the child.

Once a parent has identified a problem area(s)—for example, anger control, procrastination, hectic week problem—the focus shifts to strategies to eliminate such obstacles to change. It is important to note that the problems identified for improvement do not need to be solved in their entirety to move forward. As long as a parent is able to demonstrate some improvement in the designated area(s), it is reasonable to move on to subsequent stages of this intervention. It is advisable, however, to arrange

with the parent(s) a periodic review of progress overcoming the problems they have identified as barriers to
change.

Chapter 2—*Are Your Parenting Attitudes Helpful or
Harmful?*: At this stage I use Table 2–1, "Rational and
Irrational Parenting Attitudes," to focus the discussion. I
ask parents to review this table, disclose their specific
areas of irrational thinking, and then work on ways to
eliminate such attitudes/beliefs. I also review the advan-
tages of adhering to a rational parenting philosophy and
the disadvantages of clinging to irrational beliefs about
an oppositional child.

It is important to convey to parents that they are not
to strive for perfection in ridding themselves of irrational
beliefs, because no human being is ever totally free from
irrational thinking, self-defeating emotions, and dysfunctional behaviors. Rational thinking (and the more moderate emotions and behaviors that flow from such thinking) is a goal to be pursued continuously but not
perfectionistically. As long as a parent is operating primarily within a framework of rational thought, the chances
of helping a child function better are improved. To help
parents internalize rational parenting beliefs, a daily review of the coping statements listed at the end of this
chapter should be encouraged.

Chapter 3—*Positive Reinforcement Techniques*: At
this stage I begin formal parent training in child manage-

ment methods. One of the main goals of this phase is to introduce parents to the skill of differential attention (Forehand and McMahon 1981), that is, responding enthusiastically to good, appropriate, competent behavior and thinking in the child, and ignoring bad, inappropriate, incompetent behavior and thinking as much as possible. This chapter teaches parents a variety of positive reinforcement techniques to encourage cooperative behavior from the child. To support skill development in this area, I often show parents a twenty-five-minute video entitled "The Art of Effective Praising" (Webster-Stratton 1984), which illustrates the multifaceted nature of good praising technique. Many similar videos are now commercially available.

At this point parents are also helped to review the overall emotional, behavioral, and moral tone of their home, to start using all of the positive social reinforcement techniques discussed in this chapter, and to structure the child's day so that chores and tasks are completed before access to daily privileges is allowed.

Chapter 4—*Penalties for Noncompliance, Defiance, and Aggression*: In this step there is further discussion of the skill of differential attention, mainly as it pertains to ignoring inappropriate behaviors. Once parents grasp the essential elements of ignoring, I move on to train them in the variations of the time-out procedure discussed in this chapter. The use of Figure 4–2, "The Parental Command–Consequence Procedure," facilitates learning of the time-out technique. At this point I also often show an eighteen-minute video entitled "Limit Setting" (Kavanagh et al. 1991), which shows examples of parents setting limits, using time-out, and following through on consequences. Before parents use penalty techniques, it is important for them to review the penalty skills ground rules detailed in this chapter.

Chapter 5—*Self-Control Skills, Part I: Building Thinking Skills*: At this point I invite the child back to the sessions and begin to introduce him or her to flexible, rational thinking. For children 7 to 11 years of age I am usually able to help them see to some extent why their irrational beliefs are irrational (unhelpful). I also am able, by means of the techniques described by Bernard and Joyce (1984), to encourage many children to begin using rational coping statements to develop "psychological armor" against life's insults and provocations. For younger children 4 to 6 years of age I simply teach them to repeat simple coping statements when they are frustrated and praise them when they do so. There are a number of children in my caseload running around town practicing "I can handle it," "It could be worse," "I'm a worthwhile kid" types of thoughts to their benefit. I do not attempt self-control training with children 2 to 3 years of age. Instead I rely primarily on teaching parents behavior modification and relationship-enhancing techniques to help the child improve his or her behavior.

During this phase parents are present as I conduct individual psychotherapy with the child. The parents listen to my dialogue with the child so they can learn how to coach him or her in the use of rational thinking at home. The presence of the parents encourages them to become my "agents of skill generalization," and they become able to help the child use better thinking skills outside of sessions.

Chapter 6—*Self-Control Skills, Part II: Building Verbalization Skills*: At this stage of self-control training I evaluate the child's current feelings vocabulary and identify the specific emotions he or she needs help in identifying and expressing. I also introduce the ideas of first and second feelings and preferential speech and encourage the child to start practicing these skills in difficult or frustrating situations or when trying to express opinions. The parental task at this phase is to work with the child on identifying and expressing feelings and to begin using all of the verbal skill-building methods described in this chapter with special emphasis on helping the child learn the art of preferential thinking and speech.

Chapter 7—*Self-Control Skills, Part III: Building Impulse-Control, Problem-Solving, and Tease-Tolerance Skills*: This final stage of self-control training encourages the child to memorize and utilize a specific problem-solving formula to reduce his seemingly automatic aggressive responses and to improve his impulse-control and problem-solving capabilities. To help the child learn this six-step formula it is advisable to collect several examples of problems he has recently encountered and conduct an after-the-fact review of these difficult situations using the formula outline you want the child to learn. At this point my four-step tease-tolerance technique is also reviewed and practiced with the child. As in all prior self-control training sessions, the parents are present to observe and to learn the techniques in the hope that they will then be better able to coach and support the child's self-control efforts at home.

Chapter 8—*Monitoring Progress*: This final chapter is used to help parents identify specific social and behavioral goals for the child and, through the use of the high-priority skills workplan, to map the multiple methods of influence that will be used to help the child develop more competent behaviors, social skills, and attitudes. At this point I often use a session to write the skills workplan collaboratively with parents and to reinforce the need for parents to use the plan vigorously and consistently.

This chapter also presents a structured method for monitoring the child's progress. The main technique discussed is a parental monitoring procedure that simultaneously reinforces the child's social and behavioral goals, helps the child develop the capacity for accurate self-reflection, and provides a forum for parent and child to discuss solutions to problems. Once implemented, this daily monitoring exercise between parent and child becomes the centerpiece of the child's aftercare plan. At this point I often initiate termination with the understanding that the parents will continue to work with the child's teacher and other involved professionals as long as necessary to manage the child's recovery. Parents are advised to call me for booster sessions as needed.

This parent training intervention does not always produce the desired outcome. Unfortunately, some children remain embedded in oppositional, defiant, and aggressive modes of relatedness. In these cases I first consider the possibility of longer term outpatient treatment for the child and his family. If further outpatient treatment is not advisable, I usually recommend referral to a more structured level of care, such as a day treatment or residential treatment program.

There is nothing absolute or dogmatic in these guidelines. Clinicians should feel free to adapt or modify any aspect of my approach based on their clinical judgment and the individual treatment needs of each child and his parents. Nevertheless, for a substantial number of children who present with disruptive behavior disorders, the parent training and child self-control methods described in this book generally—though not always—yield rapid behavioral improvement for the child and a positive therapeutic experience for the entire family.

Suggested Reading

Procrastination

Bernard, M. (1991). *Procrastinate Later!* Melbourne: Schwartz and Wilkinson.

This book presents Dr. Bernard's magnetic theory of procrastination. This theory is based on nine major factors that push or repel you away from hard tasks and one key factor that pulls or draws you away from the work that you need to do. Dr. Bernard also discusses, in considerable detail, the various addictions, fantasies, and self-lies that produce procrastination. This book will provide you with insight into the psychology of procrastination, as well as twenty-five specific self-help techniques to overcome it.

Ellis, A., and Knaus, W. (1977). *Overcoming Procrastination.* New York: New American Library.

This book does a remarkable job of examining psychological factors that can produce the behavior known as procrastination. In their discussion, Drs. Ellis and Knaus show how self-downing, low frustration tolerance, hostility, perfectionism, anxiety, guilt, shame, or depression may lead to avoidance of tasks and responsibilities. This book also illuminates many of the irrational beliefs that contribute to procrastination. If your procrastination does not prevent you from finishing this book, you will learn a variety of cognitive, emotive, and behavioral techniques to overcome the problems noted above and increase your work productivity at home and at the office.

Anger Management

Barrish, H., and Barrish, I. J. (1989). *Managing and Understanding Parental Anger.* Kansas City, KS: Westport. (Now available directly from the authors, 1(913) 491-4343.)

This is a great book and the one I most often recommend to parents to reduce and prevent overly angry responses to their children. In a clear and concise manner the authors teach parents the major unhelpful beliefs that create intense anger toward children and offer specific thinking remedies designed to lower anger. Although it is only forty-three pages in length, you will find this book packed with advice that will help improve the quality of your relationship with your child.

Ellis A., and Tafrate, R. C. (1997). *How to Control Your Anger Before It Controls You.* Secaucus, NJ: Carol/Birch Lane.

When it comes to a discussion of anger, this book leaves no stone unturned. Throughout the discussion, Drs. Ellis and Tafrate systematically show how you create and maintain your anger by holding rigidly to self-angering philosophies about other people and the world. This book will help you detect and dispute your self-angering philosophies and beliefs, and it will teach you numerous ways to think, feel, and act your way out of an overly angry outlook on life.

Hauck, P. A. (1974). *Overcoming Frustration and Anger.* Philadelphia: Westminster. (Now available through Westminster/John Knox in Louisville, KY.)

This is another good book to help you learn about the sources of your anger and to change yourself into a less angry person. In the discussion Dr. Hauck shows you the complete psychological sequences of getting angry. He also shows how to deal with self-righteous anger and how to stop being so blaming of others. The book concludes with nine specific guidelines for overcoming frustration and anger.

Rational Living and Parenting

Ellis, A. (1988). *How to Stubbornly Refuse to Make Yourself Miserable About Anything—Yes, Anything!* Secaucus, NJ: Lyle Stuart.

This is a book you should stubbornly refuse to put down until you have finished it. It will give you many insights into the ways in which you needlessly disturb yourself over a variety of life problems. The self-help techniques it contains will also help you gain control of your emotional destiny so that you can maximally enjoy life and have as little emotional pain as possible.

Ellis, A., and Harper, R. A. (1997). *A Guide to Rational Living*,
    3rd rev. ed. North Hollywood, CA: Wilshire.

This guide to rational living is one of the most widely read
self-help books in the world. In it Drs. Ellis and Harper discuss in detail ten irrational beliefs that cause human psychological disturbance. If you study this book carefully and actively model its self-helping philosophies around your child,
you will be showing him or her how not to become an emo-
tionally disturbed individual.

Hauck, P. (1967). *The Rational Management of Children*. Roslyn
    Heights, NY: Libra. (Now available through Libra in San
    Diego, CA.)

This book will teach you many ways to promote psychological health in your child. Dr. Hauck discusses the common
erroneous beliefs about child management, as well as specific guidelines to help children conquer fears of failure and
fears of rejection and ridicule. He also discusses ways that
you can help your child overcome states of anger and depression and offers sound advice on methods of discipline.

References

Barkley, R. (1997). *Defiant Children: A Clinician's Manual for Assessment and Parent Training.* New York: Guilford.

Bernard, M., and Joyce, M. (1984). *Rational-Emotive Therapy with Children and Adolescents.* New York: Wiley.

Bloomquist, M. (1996). *Skills Training for Children with Behavior Disorders.* New York: Guilford.

Breen, M., and Altepeter, T. (1990). *Disruptive Behavior Disorders in Children.* New York: Guilford.

Chess, S., and Thomas, A. (1991). Temperament. In *Child and Adolescent Psychiatry: A Comprehensive Textbook,* ed. M. Lewis, pp. 145–159. Baltimore: Williams & Wilkins.

Ellis, A. (1975). *How to Live with a Neurotic.* Hollywood, CA: Wilshire.

——— (1994). *Reason and Emotion in Psychotherapy.* New York: Birch Lane.

Ellis, A., and Dryden, W. (1987). *The Practice of Rational Emotive Therapy.* New York: Springer.

Forehand, R., and Long, N. (1996). *Parenting the Strong-Willed Child.* Chicago: Contemporary Books.

Forehand, R., and McMahon, R. (1981). *Helping the Noncompliant Child.* New York: Guilford.

Huber, C., and Baruth, L. (1989). *Rational-Emotive Family Therapy: A Systems Perspective.* New York: Springer.

Kavanagh, K., Frey, J., and Larsen, D., producers (1991). *Growing Opportunities School-Age Series Part 2: Limit Setting* (videotape). Eugene, OR: Castalia.

Kazdin, A. (1985). *Treatment of Antisocial Behavior in Children and Adolescents.* Homewood, IL: Dorsey.

———— (1994). *Behavior Modification in Applied Settings,* 5th ed. Pacific Grove, CA: Brooks/Cole.

Kendall, P., and Braswell, L. (1993). *Cognitive-Behavioral Therapy for Impulsive Children,* 2nd ed. New York: Guilford.

King, R., and Noshpitz, J. (1991). Conduct disorder. In *Pathways of Growth: Essentials of Child Psychiatry,* vol. 2: *Psychopathology,* pp. 400–452. New York: Wiley.

Lewis, D. (1991). Conduct disorder. In *Child and Adolescent Psychiatry: A Comprehensive Textbook,* ed. M. Lewis, pp. 561–573. Baltimore: Williams & Wilkins.

Nelson, W., and Finch, A. (1996). *Cognitive-Behavioral Therapy for Aggressive Children: Therapist Manual.* Ardmore, PA: Workbook Publishing.

Patterson, G., Reid, J., Jones, R., and Conger, R. (1975). *A Social Learning Approach to Family Intervention.* Eugene, OR: Castalia.

Porter-Thal, N. (1994). *Parents, Children and Divorce,* 4th ed. Fort Meyers, FL: The Training Company.

Strayhorn, J. M. (1988). *The Competent Child: An Approach to Psychotherapy and Preventive Mental Health.* New York: Guilford.

———— (1995). *The Competence Approach to Parenting.* Wexford, PA: Strayhorn Publications.

Webster-Stratton, C., producer (1984). *The Parents and Children Series Praise and Rewards Program Part I: The Art of Effective Praising* (videotape). Seattle, WA: Seth Enterprises.

Wenning, K., Nathan, P., and King, S. (1993). Mood disorders in children with oppositional defiant disorder: a pilot study. *American Journal of Orthopsychiatry* 63:295–299.

Windell, J. (1994). *8 Weeks to a Well-Behaved Child.* New York: Macmillan.

Index

Aggression. *See* Oppositional, defiant behavior
Altepeter, T., 6
Anger
  expression of, 121
  management of,
    bibliography, 176–177
  parental, 8
  self-control skills, 122–126
Anxiety, penalties, 72–73
Attitudes, choices in, self-control skills, 141–143

Barkley, R., 22, 57, 62, 76, 81, 85
Baruth, L., 34
Bedtime behavior, penalties, 89, 92–95

Behavior
  bedtime, penalties, 89, 92–95
  choices in, self-control skills, 141–143
  morning, penalties, 89, 90–92
  social learning principles, 26–28
Behavioral skills, self-control skills, 131–144. *See also* Self-control skills (behavioral skills)
Bernard, M., 101, 102
Bibliography, 175–178
Blaming, change obstacle, 14–15
Bloomquist, M., 127
Books, positive reinforcement, 52

Braswell, L., 135, 155
Breen, M., 6

Catastrophe, parenting
    attitudes, 37–39
Catastrophe scale, 38
Change
    clinician guidelines, 167–168
    key points in, 28–29
    obstacles to, 13–16
    parental, 7–12
    preparation for, 4–5
    types of, 3–4
Cheating, irrational beliefs, 106
Chess, S., 20
Child self-report, skills
    workplan, 154
Choice
    attitudes, self-control skills,
        141–143
    positive reinforcement, 50
Clinicians, guidelines for, 163–173
Communications, penalties, 87–
    89. See also Self-control
    skills (verbalization skills)
Compliance training periods,
    positive reinforcement
    techniques, 57–59
Conflict
    parental, 10–11
    resolution of, positive
        reinforcement, 50–51
Consistency, failure in, 20. See
    also Inconsistency
Coping statements, for parents,
    42–44

Daily feelings diary, self-
    control skills, 127–128

Defiance, irrational beliefs, 104
Defiant behavior. See
    Oppositional, defiant
    behavior
Demandingness, parenting
    attitudes, 34–37
Denial, parenting attitudes, 37–
    40
Destructiveness, irrational
    beliefs, 108–109
Direction giving, positive
    reinforcement, 49–50
Disappointment, expression of,
    119
Divorce, positive
    reinforcement, 53
Dryden, W., 33, 37

Ellis, A., 15, 33, 34, 37, 101
Embarrassment, expression of,
    120
Envy, expression of, 120
Ethics, positive reinforcement,
    54
Extinction burst, ignoring
    technique, 75

Fear, change obstacle, 15
Feelings, expression of, 117–122
Finch, A., 135
Flexibility, self-control skills
    (thinking skills), 99–101
Forehand, R., 19, 26, 27, 51,
    74, 75, 80, 169
Frustration
    expression of, 119–120
    irrational beliefs, 107–108
    parenting attitudes, 39–40
    penalties, 72

Goals identification, progress
    monitoring, 147–148, 149
Guilt
    expression of, 121–122
    penalties, 72–73

Harmful behavior, positive
    reinforcement, 54–55
High-priority skills workplan,
    progress monitoring, 148,
    150–154
Huber, C., 34

Ignoring technique, penalties,
    74–76
Impulse-control
    clinician guidelines, 171–
    172
    self-control skills, 133–138
Inconsistency, change obstacle,
    15–16. *See also*
    Consistency
Irrationality
    of child, 21–22
    parenting attitudes, 34–42
    self-control skills (thinking
    skills), 101–109

Jealousy, expression of, 120–
    121
Joyce, M., 101, 102

Kavanagh, K., 84, 170
Kazdin, A., 17, 19, 75
Kendall, P., 135, 155
King, R., 51

Learning, social learning
    principles, 26–28

Lewis, D., 17
Long, N., 51
Lying, irrational beliefs, 105

Marital relationship, positive
    reinforcement, 53, 60–
    62
McMahon, R., 19, 26, 27, 74,
    75, 80, 169
Media, violence, positive
    reinforcement, 51–52
Minimization, parenting
    attitudes, 38
Monitoring. *See* Progress
    monitoring
Morality, positive
    reinforcement, 54
Morning behavior, penalties,
    89, 90–92

Nagging, threatening,
    screaming/spanking
    syndrome, described,
    22–26
Negative attention syndrome,
    17, 18
Nelson, W., 135
Nightly review, positive
    reinforcement techniques,
    59–60
Noshpitz, J., 51

Oppositional, defiant behavior
    causes of, 16–26
    facts about, 5–6
Oppositional behavior,
    irrational beliefs, 104–
    105
Optimism, parental, 10

Parenting attitudes, 31–44
  bibliography, 177–178
  clinician guidelines, 168
  coping statements, 42–44
  importance of, 33–34
  key points in, 44
  rationality, 34–42
Parent report, progress
  monitoring, 157
Parents
  change in, 7–12
  stress on, 21
Past problems, avoidance of,
  positive reinforcement,
  53–54
Patterson, G., 22
Penalties, 69–95
  bedtime behavior, 89, 92–95
  clinician guidelines, 169–170
  communications, 87–89
  effectiveness of, 71
  ground rules for, 71–74
  ignoring technique, 74–76
  key points, 95
  morning behavior, 89, 90–92
  time-out, 76–87. *See also*
    Time-out
Playfulness, parental, 11
Porter-Thal, N., 53
Positive reinforcement, 45–68
  clinician guidelines, 168–169
  key points, 68
  privileges and rewards, 64–
    67
  shaping the tone, 47–55
  social learning principles, 27
  techniques of, 55–63
Praise, positive reinforcement
  techniques, 55–63

Preferential communication,
  self-control skills, 116–117
Privileges, positive
  reinforcement, 64–67
Problem-solving skills
  of child, 21–22
  clinician guidelines, 171–172
  self-control skills, 133–138
Procrastination
  bibliography, 175–176
  change obstacle, 13
Progress monitoring, 145–161
  clinician guidelines, 172–173
  goals identification, 147–148,
    149
  key points, 161
  self-reflection, 155–159
  skills workplan, 148, 150–154
  tips in, 159–161
Property destruction, irrational
  beliefs, 108–109
Psychological problems,
  parental, 9–10
Punishment
  excessive use of, 19
  failure to administer
    appropriately, 17, 19
  social learning principles, 28

Rage, irrational beliefs, 103
Rationality
  bibliography, 177–178
  parenting attitudes, 34–42
  self-control skills (thinking
    skills), 101–109
Reinforcement, social learning
  principles, 27–28
Respect, positive
  reinforcement, 53

Rewards
  failure to give, 17
  of inappropriate behavior, 22
  positive reinforcement, 64–67
Rigidity, self-control skills
  (thinking skills), 99–101
Role model
  parental, 9
  positive reinforcement, 48
Rules, positive reinforcement,
  48–49

Sadness
  of child, 12
  expression of, 118
Screaming/spanking phase, 25
Self-control skills (behavioral
  skills), 131–144
  attitudes, choices in, 141–143
  clinician guidelines, 171–172
  impulse-control and
    problem-solving, 133–138
  key points, 143–144
  tease-tolerance, 138–141
Self-control skills (thinking
  skills), 97–110
  clinician guidelines, 170–171
  flexibility, 99–101
  irrational beliefs, 101–109
    cheating, 106
    defiance, 104
    frustration, 107–108
    lying, 105
    oppositional behavior, 104–105
    property destruction, 108–109

  rage, 103
  stealing, 106–107
  key points, 109–110
Self-control skills (verbalization
  skills), 111–129
  acting out, alternative to,
    126–127
  anger, 122–126
  clinician guidelines, 171
  daily feelings diary, 127–128
  feelings expression, 117–122
  key points, 129
  pleasant conversation, 114–115
  preferential communication,
    116–117
  talking it out, 128–129
Self-reflection, encouragement
  of, progress monitoring,
  155–159
Self-report, of child, skills
  workplan, 154
Shame, expression of, 121
Shaping the tone, positive
  reinforcement, 47–55
Skills workplan, progress
  monitoring, 148, 150–154
Social learning principles,
  described, 26–28
Special time activity, positive
  reinforcement techniques,
  62–63
Spouse. See Marital relationship
Stealing, irrational beliefs, 106–107
Strayhorn, J. M., 18, 52, 59, 77,
  151, 153, 157
Stress
  on child, 20–21
  on parent, 20–21

Talking it out, self-control
skills, 128–129
Tease-tolerance
clinician guidelines, 171–172
self-control skills, 138–141
Television, violence, positive
reinforcement, 51–52
Temperament, of child, 20–21
Theft, irrational beliefs, 106–107
Thinking skills, self-control,
97–110. *See also* Self-
control skills (thinking
skills)
Thomas, A., 20
Threatening phase, 24
Time
change obstacle, 13–14
parent/child relationship, 11
Time-out, 76–89
child's refusal to go, 82–87
child's refusal to leave, 87
communications, 87–89
penalties, 73
procedures, 76–82
social learning principles, 28

Timing, penalties, 73
Trashing, parenting attitudes,
40–41

Unconditional acceptance,
parenting attitudes,
41–42

Verbalization skills, self-
control, 111–129. *See also*
Self-control skills
(verbalization skills)
Videos, positive reinforcement,
52
Violence, media, positive
reinforcement, 51–52

Webster-Stratton, C., 169
Wenning, K., 12
Windell, J., 83
Worry
of child, 12
expression of, 118–119
Worshiping others, parenting
attitudes, 41

ABOUT THE AUTHOR

Kenneth Wenning received his MSW (1980) and Ph.D. (1988) from the Smith College School for Social Work in Northampton, Massachusetts. For the past twenty years he has specialized in the evaluation and treatment of children who are oppositional, defiant, and aggressive. Dr. Wenning maintains a private practice of child and family treatment in Hamden, Connecticut.